AF791469

MICRO-TEACHING

Technique and Practice

MICRO-TEACHING

Technique and Practice

Jessie S. Modi
M.Sc.(Chem.), M.A.(Psychology), M.Ed., Ph.D.(Education)
Department of Education,
Patna University, Patna

SHIPRA
SHIPRA

All rights reserved. No part of this work may be reproduced, stored in a retrieval system or transmitted in any form or by any means, electronic, mechanical, photocopying, recording or otherwise without the prior written permission of the copyright owner and the publishers.

(2017, 2013, First Published in 2010)

Rs. 850; US$ 34

ISBN: 978- 81-7541-536-2

2020 Impression

Micro-Teaching: Technique and Practice

© Author

Published by:
SHIPRA PUBLICATIONS
LG 18-19, Pankaj Central Market,
I.P. Ext., Patparganj, Delhi 110092, India
Ph.: +91 11 22235152/6152
Email: info@shiprapublication.com
Website: www.shiprapublication.com

Preface

The basic characteristic of a good teacher is her ability to communicate. It is this need of the student that the teacher should be able to reach out and strike, through the minds of her pupils. This is to be done in such a way that, it brings about an insight of what is being taught. A conscious and dedicated teacher lives through all these stages while she teaches her pupils. Whenever a student rushes to class or longs to attend any teachers' class, it is for the simple reason that the communicating language and thoughts of the teacher is in tune with the level of understanding and grasping of the student. A teacher who is simple in her delivery of the matter she teaches in class, is more appreciated than a teacher who may be intelligent and full of knowledge, complex concepts but unable, to simplify and reach out to students.

Every teacher consciously or unconsciously plans to teach, in the best possible manner she thinks and understands, which will be suitable to the students. This book is an attempt to make teachers understand how teaching can be made more simple, once you master the skills of teaching. I have dealt with the concept and technique of 'Microteaching' in the First Chapter. The Second Chapter helps to understand skills. In the Third chapter the planning of a micro-lesson and its detail steps are explained. The next Chapter takes questioning as one of its skill and gives the exact planning and feedback as it is conducted in the class with a unit/ lesson as an example. I have tried to make its application possible using the rating scale and discussing the rated value. Also a systematic stepwise explanation which is easy to follow and very practical is given in the chapter.

The purpose of this book was felt while observing Teacher Educators rush through the theoretical part of microteaching and assuming that the students have understood and will be able to develop skills by their efforts of listening to the 'rushed through' lecture on microteaching. The practical aspect was the weak point and how to plan and proceed was a big question mark. Microteaching has become an important part of the B.Ed syllabus and M.Ed. internship programmes. While conducting microteaching sessions at the school level for teachers of Kendriya Vidyalayas at Banaras, other private schools in Patna and at the orientation session of the Lecturers at ASC, Patna University, I found the hesitation and the ego which initially prevented the teachers from planning the unit according to the said skill.

Teachers in general feel they are experts at teaching and can reach every mind that they have to mould and help build thinking. This is a positive essential belief, every teacher needs to possess. Practically it was found that they were not able to plan a five-six minute lesson focused on one skill. During the process the concept and method was cleared and each one was helped to plan and go through the practical aspect of it, they did well and understood how a particular skill could be used and exposed at its best.

Micro-teaching is an effective technique to develop teaching skills in Teachers. I do hope this book will further help in bringing more insights for teaching and useful for all types of teachers.

Acknowledgements

The usefulness of 'Microteaching' as an effective technique, to develop teaching skills in teachers, was felt from the time I joined the Teacher Training College. But how to use this technique to make the teachers under training and full time teachers actually enhance their teaching, was a difficult thought then. It became possible when I joined the Department of Education, Patna University. I was thinking of some programme for teachers. I had a discussion with Dr. U.N.Singh the then Assistant Commissioner KV Patna Region who encouraged me to conduct a 'workshop on Microteaching' for their teachers. The observation and feedback left a feeling of achievement and I was motivated further by Mrs Bisarya EO KV Patna Region to conduct more of this workshop for their teachers. The feedback was always positive after these sessions and left a pleasant feeling. I then thought of giving the benefits of my workshop to other school teachers. I requested the private schools in Patna to allow me to conduct the workshop for them. I wish to thank the Principals of these schools specially the Principal and Rector of St Xavier's School Patna.

Dr A. K. Gupta, the then Director ASC P.U. was also encouraging and had the confidence in me that I could do wonders by such a workshop for the lecturers at the Orientation Course at ASC P.U. I wish to say a thankyou to him for his encouragement and faith in me.

As I wanted to reach out to more and more teachers, I thought writing this book could help me achieve this at a faster rate. My acknowledgement will be incomplete if I do not thank Sister Sylvie from Patna Women's College who supported me in my endeavor of writing this book.

Content

Chapter 1

Micro-Teaching

MEANING AND CONCEPT

Micro-teaching is an effective technique to develop teaching skills in Teachers. The skills are defined in terms of teaching behaviours and the objectives towards which such behaviours are aimed which will bring about a desired change in pupils. It was invented in the mid 1960's at Stanford University by Dr. Dwight Allen and this method has helped teachers acquire skills for teaching.

In this method one Teacher teaches and a group of 5-10 pupils (also teachers in a mock classroom situation) observe the teachers performance of teaching and give a feedback keeping in mind the particular skill under consideration.

The student teacher plans a short lesson in which he demonstrates the use of skill. The lessons/unit makes use of teaching skills that can be taught, evaluated, predicted, controlled and understood (Passi-1976) The teacher applies teaching skills to carefully prepared lessons in a planned series of five to ten minutes, encounters a small group of real students, often with an opportunity to observe the result on videotape. (Bush-1968) It is an organized form of practice teaching and helps in making a teacher effective in his preparation to deliver the planned lesson to the class.

In the original process a teacher was asked to prepare a short lesson (usually 20 minutes) for a small group of learners who may not be his own students. This was videotaped using VHS. After the lesson, the teacher, her teaching colleagues, a master teacher and the students together viewed the videotape and commented on, what they saw happening, referencing the teachers learning objectives. Seeing the video and getting comments from the colleagues and students provided teachers with an often intense, under the microscope view of their teaching (From Wikipedia, the free encyclopedia)

Micro-teaching as practiced in the training programme of teachers is a "scaled down teaching encounter" in which a teacher teaches a small unit of the lesson to a group of 5 to 10 pupils for a small period of time (5 to 10 minutes) Such a situation offers a helpful setting for an experienced or inexperienced teacher to acquire new teaching skills and to refine old ones.

The teaching skills are defined in terms of teaching behaviours and the objectives which determine this behaviour. The student-teacher also decides the unit in such a way that there is maximum scope to demonstrate the decided skill.

PHASES OF MICROTEACHING

Every microteaching session if analysed, it will be found that it proceeds through three phases.

1. Knowledge Acquisition Phase
2. Skill Acquisition Phase
3. Transfer Phase

In the **Knowledge Acquisition Phase** the student teacher understands the various skills and its components. He also understands how these components are going to bring about the required changes in the teaching behaviour. The knowledge of the rationale behind the skill and its role in the classroom plays an important role.. Reading relevant literature, observing the class-demonstration of fellow student-teachers, analyzing the use of the components in the unit, helps in this knowledge acquisition phase. Discussing these after analysis, and trying to build the components of the skill further helps in modelling the components, of the skill. This can then define and present the skill clearly and specifically.

In the **Skill Acquisition Phase** the student selects a unit and plans it according to the components of the skill. He then demonstrates the unit and gets a feedback and then he re-plans the same unit and re-teaches it till he acquires the level of mastery.

In this phase, two parts play an important role:

1. Setting *and*
2. Feedback.

In ***'Setting'*** care is taken to have the proper physical structure like the size of the class, duration of the lesson, presence of a supervisor, interested pupils who will teach the unit using the skill and also those who will give proper feedback..

In ***'Feedback'*** the observing student teachers are carefully analyzing the use of the components in the unit taught and then giving a feedback to the Teacher teaching.(If rating scales are used then a high rating or a low rating has to be explained so that the trainee teacher receiving the feedback is able to understand his shortcomings in the use of the component of the skill and thus can rectify it.) *Proper feedback is the essential ingredient to master the skills of teaching.*

In the **Transfer Phase** the skills with their components after mastering, are integrated and transferred to real classroom situation teaching. This transition takes place easily and the skills practiced during the microteaching sessions are transferred smoothly to regular teaching.

PROCESS/STEPS OF MICROTEACHING

A microteaching session is carried out in a mock classroom situation where there are five to ten students only. In the teacher training programme these students in the mock classroom could be the trainee colleagues and the teacher practicing the skill too, is one of the student-teachers. This class could also be observed by a Supervisor/videotaped/audio-taped. The feed-back is then analysed by the group with the Supervisor for guidance and help. He also reinforces the comments and indicates instances of the effective use of the skills and also suggests if the skill could be used anywhere in the unit more than/or better than the manner in which it has been used. This is then followed by the re-planning of the same unit by the teacher and reteaching it to the same set of students. Once again it is followed by a re-feedback and the process goes on till the mastery of the skill is attained.

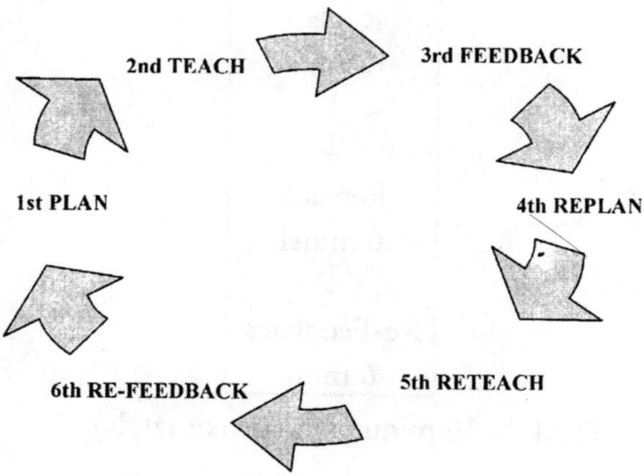

The whole process *begins with: orienting the students about microteaching, discussing the teaching skills and its components followed by the presentation of a model lesson.* This process is then put to the student-teachers who then go about it, as shown in the follow chart below:

The microteaching cycle takes about 36 minutes on an average (shown in the flow chart below).

Plan l
↓
Teach
6 mins
1
↓
Feedback
6 mins
1
↓
Replan
12 mins
1
↓
Reteach
6 minsl
↓
Re-Feedback
6 mins

TOTAL = 36 minutes (approximately)

PREPARING THE CLASS TO USE MICROTEACHING

Whenever microteaching sessions are held it is essential to introduce the concept, explain the essential steps and the focus on developing the specific skill which needs to be stressed, Also the idea behind the method is to develop the skills of the teacher who is practicing teaching by this technique. It is not a method for increasing the understanding of the unit taught to the mock group acting as a class of school students or increasing the general knowledge(in the unit's content) of the mock group. Hence these lessons are special and they can be summed up as special for the following reasons.

- A short unit of a topic (lesson) of about five to six minutes is selected.
- One skill is planned/used/practiced
- The focus is on developing specific skill
- The experienced/inexperienced teacher acquires new teaching skills and modifies the old ones.
- The performance results are immediate in the form of feedback/re-feedback.

SELECTING THE UNIT, TEACHING AND FEEDBACK

The above cited points again make us focus on the concept of microteaching which helps us to be attentive on specified aspects of our behaviour. After understanding the process and knowing the skill and its components, a student-teacher selects a unit from the lesson which is suitable to expose the particular skill (single) to a maximum, planned for duration of five to six minute. When this unit is taught to the mock classroom (fellow student-teachers) the focused view has to be, to become a skillful teacher and concentrate on ones own method of utilizing the skill to put forward the topic, rather than with an idea that we are going to drill the unit into the heads of the student-teacher. The feedback should be objective and unbiased so that the student- teacher is able to actually see the scope of improving the method of teaching the unit better, with an improvement in utilization of the skill.

TEACHING IN A REGULAR CLASS/REGULAR PERIOD

In a classroom the teaching situation is different. The classroom period is of duration of 30-35 minutes. A teacher plans a lesson of 20-25 minutes. Teaching in a normal classroom is complex because we use a number of skills together during the transaction of the unit i.e. we are integrating a number of skills into the unit.

ADVANTAGES

The advantages of Micro-teaching are as under:

- Can be practiced in the Institute/College class itself.
- The Lesson/Topic is broken into smaller unit.
- Only one skill is practiced at a time.
- Less Time is needed for the whole process.
- Every one observing, follows the trainee performance closely to give a feedback.
- Immediate feedback and correction for improvement.
- Objectives are clear.
- Programme individualized and not bound by any particular course structure.

- Suitable for all subjects.
- Simplifies complex teaching process.
- Efficiency in terms of time.
- Mock classroom situation with trainees as real students.
- Training facilities and classroom present.
- Provides teaching in simplified situations.
- Helps analyse how a unit could be taught best using relevant skills to the unit.
- Practically practicing by self in the session helps learn the use of skill but also viewing a video-recorded version.
- It can also help to learn on one's own.
- Focuses on teaching behaviour.
- It does not require any equipment as such if its not present.
- More important is the persons who will give the correct feedback.
- Parameter of disturbance, inattentiveness, indiscipline is controlled.

DISADVANTAGE

The disadvantages of Micro-teaching are:

- Very expensive, if videotape facilities are used.
- Needs time for understanding and assimilating and using in regular class lessons.
- Only one skill so not a whole lesson/chapter.
- Micro-teaching session not same as classroom teaching session.

- Organisation and class management is not the simultaneous focus as in classroom situation.
- Concentration is only on relevant teacher behaviour.
- Observers and Supervisors also need training.

Chapter 2

Teaching Skills

MEANING AND ITS IMPORTANCE IN TEACHING

Teaching skills are strategies teachers use to enable children to learn something 'worthwhile' like facts, skills, values, concepts, how to live harmoniously with ones fellows, attitudes or some other outcomes thought to be desirable. Also a skill has to be acknowledged by those competent to judge like teachers, teacher trainers, inspectors and learners themselves. The skill is also such that it can be repeated .It may not be in the same form but it is frequent rather than a chance occurrence(like a hit-or-miss basis).

Some teachers may be very skilful but may not be very good at articulating it, using a language. "One problem encountered in defining teaching skill is that though in some context the term 'skill' has a good connotation. It attracts adulation, is a gift of the few, the result of years of practice or the mark of an expert. But in other circumstances, it is looked down upon, regarded as mechanical, like a rude technician rather than an artist. For example, we tend, for instance to admire a surgeons skill or that of a tennis player. Both may have the same years of dedicated practice, but the intellectual nature of the knowledge and understanding required by the surgeon is vastly more exacting than that required by the sportsman. Skill makes you an expert and comes from practiced ability.

Where the imagination is involved, even finer distinctions exist. A sculptor would probably be disappointed to read a report that described his latest masterpiece as an example of skill. He would expect eulogies to contain words like 'artistic' and 'creative'. For those who liken teachers more to expressive artists than to surgeons, the very term 'skill' may be seen as belittling, reducing creative endeavor to mechanical crudity. It is difficult to dry-clean the term of these emotional association with other kinds of human enterprise.

This uncertainty about the proper standing of the notion of skill when applied to teaching is partly explained by the varied nature of the teacher's job. Pressing the right button on a tape recorder, or writing legibly on the blackboard require modest competence, and are things which most people could learn with only a little practice. Responding to a disruptive 19 year old, or knowing how to explain a difficult concept to children of different ages and abilities by choosing the right language, register appropriate examples and analogies, and reading the many cues which signal understanding or bewilderment, require years of practice as well as considerable intelligence and insight. Although the term 'interpersonal skills is quite widespread, there is still some reluctance to classify human relationships in this way." (Wragg Edward. Conrad – Primary Teaching Skills)

Today the demand from a teacher is a high level of professional competence. Professional competence would include rapid growth in the acquisition of knowledge, demands of the society in terms of the types of employment, leisure, accountability, wider development in the educational field and information technology as well as broadening the role of the Teacher who has to accommodate change and not only improve but also renew the old practice. An effective teacher should possess knowledge and understanding of the content of the subjects and topics being taught, as well as the ability to manage a class, explain clearly, ask intelligent and appropriate questions, and monitor and assess learning.

All these factors mentioned require combining with skill, understanding, imagination and resilience from teachers to go beyond what has already been practiced yesterday and before.

Knowledge explosion is on its upward journey and a teacher has to know his content of education and how much of it is needed at a particular age or level and what part of the content should be present. If he cannot know everything he has to find out, understand and know the process of learning by the students and how to transact this, by the teacher. The teaching strategies should encourage children to learn independently as well as in a group.

Social change and demands for qualifications at the higher level has put a tremendous pressure on the teacher. He is compelled to use the skills of teaching effectively at the basic school level so that the foundations laid are strong to face the technological and bureaucratic society. Every parent is trying to fit in his child and the child too is trying to fit himself, into it.

Teachers, hence have to be skillful not only in terms of content but also in terms of setting the tone of the class, building interactions and interpersonal relation which will in turn help learning , thinking, understanding and lead to insight while observing, assimilating and accommodating what is being taught.

The demand for skillful teachers is increasing. The quality of teacher too is improving. Good teachers are keen and enthusiastic, well organized and firm, fair and stimulating, know their stuff and are interested in the welfare of the students They want to move from the traditional to progressive. Many still tend to use the traditional methods even if they know they should move towards progressive methods. We as teachers, find it easy to copy or imitate someone else, rather than try to analyse and determine newer ways to teach and learn. We have to be objective and focused not only on the transaction of the content but also on the recipient i.e. the students–how and how-much they are understanding, grasping and even assimilating and accommodating of what is being taught and put forward to them as content.

Microteaching makes use of techniques to use teaching skills in teaching small units of the lesson to the class, thereby helping to inculcate within the teacher the skills that go with the lessons/unit taught to the class. Every skill has a set of behaviour which the teacher is able to observe, understand in order to modify his behaviour according to the specified objectives. Also the observers (student-teachers giving the feedback) are able to learn behaviours of teachers which contribute to effective learning in pupils and how to improve on ones own teaching. We shall see the different skills and their components in the following unit.

DIFFERENT TEACHING SKILLS

There are many skills that go into a complete lesson/ unit. What could be suitable at what juncture in the lesson, is for the teacher to decide. In microteaching since a small unit is taken for teaching, the unit should be such that the particular skill has a maximum scope of using the components and helps in the transaction of the unit (by the teacher), and understanding it (by the student). Thus brings about the desired change in the teacher.

In classroom teaching, the teacher generally uses skills like questioning, explanation, stimulus variation, response management, reinforcement & illustrating with examples. There are often used often during the teaching of any unit. (referred to as Core Teaching Skills.)

Below we have some skills (including the core skills) which are generally and often used while teaching different subjects for different level of students. This list below is followed by its components:

1. Questioning
2. Explanation
3. Audio-visual aids
4. Stimulus Variation
5. Reinforcement
6. Introduction of a lesson
7. Achieving closure
8. Response Management
9. Illustrating with examples
10. Narration
11. Recitation
12. Pupil Participation/Interaction
13. Dramatization
14. Classroom Management
15. Use of Black-board

COMPONENTS OF THE SKILLS

1. Skill Questioning

Questioning is a very effective method used often by a Teacher in class, during her teaching. Often we ask questions mostly after having taught a unit. Asking questions can be a useful tool in the hands of the teacher not only to introduce and build concepts but it also helps in proceeding with the topic, stimulate thinking, help understand how much the pupil knows and also be able to draw conclusions. These questions have to be planned and managed so that the teacher is able to *bring about the behavioural changes in the pupil according to the expected behaviour changes.*

Thus, the questions should be quality oriented and stimulate further process of the unit taught. This is difficult initially and focusing on the action and reaction that a question can bring about will help formulation of good questions. It may seem to be difficult initially but with practice it will become a part of the teaching process for the teacher.

The questions asked should stimulate thinking and hence questions with Yes/No as answers should be avoided as these could be just guessed answers. Many times a question has more than one answer/idea. These should be avoided as many times students remain silent wondering which answer is the expected one. So, sharper questions directed towards the expected concept/answer should be asked. Also ambiguous answers should be avoided as these fail to communicate the idea or concept. Many times lack of grammar and language also make questions ambiguous and out of focus. Hence these points should also be borne in mind. Therefore the Question should be:

- **clear, specific, and relevant.** Clear as far as the language, tense, negatives in the question is concerned. It should be specific and straight to lead to the particular answer. It should be relevant and based on the content being taught.
- **grammatically correct, accurate.** The questions should have the proper interrogation. The words, verbs and other parts of the questions should be

proper and correct and accurate. This will help to focus on the content and the accuracy based on it.

- **stimulating interest and thinking.** The question should hold the attention of the students, create an interest in knowing and understanding the question, thereby leading to think on the question asked and draw an answer.
- **seeking further information, providing lead/ sequence of thought.** The questions asked should be such that the students are thinking and wanting to know, ahead of the contents taught and the question has provoked them to go ahead in the sequence of their thoughts. It has stimulated them to think and know more about the contents.
- **helps to observe/understand.** This is a type of question which makes you see the answer to the question, form concepts from the question itself and understand what is being taught in the class.
- **forms concept, idea, relationship.** The questions help in determining the concept and the idea from the matter taught. Simultaneously the relationship in the contents or equations from the matter/statement of the content comes to the notice of the students.
- **sufficient.** Many times a large no of questions, meaning the same things are asked even before waiting for the students to answer. At other times just one question is asked and the teacher waits for the answer. Both the things are not good. If

the correct answer is not given a cue can be given and further probed with shorter questions to arrive at the answer. Depending on the need, the no of questions should be increased or decreased.

- **involves student participation.** Questions should not separate the students as individuals. They should help in making the student involved in their thinking, exchanging and discussing the answers they give to the questions.
- **have quality/assess students understanding.** As already said the questions should have quality rather than quantity and they should help the teacher teaching, assess the understanding of the unit by the students' answers and make him know the level of the students understanding of the topic he has taught.

S. No.	*Components of the skill*	*1*	*2*	*3*	*4*	*5*
1.	Question are Clear, specific, relevant				√	
2.	Grammatically correct, accurate				√	
3.	Stimulating interest and thinking			√		
4.	Seeking further information, providing lead/sequence of thought		√			
5.	Helps to observe/understand		√			
6.	Forms concept, idea, relationship			√		
7.	Sufficient		√			
8.	Involves student participation			√		
9.	Have quality/assess students understanding.				√	
	Total		6	9	12	
	Total 27/45					

2. Skill Explanation

It consists of the use of interrelated statements which help to build concepts, develop ideas and understanding of a phenomenon. These interrelated statements tell us about the causes, reasons, action-reactions and various logical steps that go in helping to build the concept in the content being taught. Many times an explanation requires a number of other relevant objects, aids, examples, showing relationships or experiences, to build up the explanation and these in turn make use of interrelated statements. Certain ideas and facts are described and related in the process of explanation to promote the understanding of the content of the unit taught.

An explanation makes use of statements grammatically correct, covering essential points of the topic, linking the subtopics in the course of the explanation, using av-aids to make the topic clear, build concepts and make the unit taught interesting.. It may also use new terms and words, with the meaning and concept clarified. An explanation can also contain questions to make the unit interactive, stimulating and thought provoking. It also helps to know how much the pupils are understanding and following your explanation. Above all, an explanation should be fluent and flowing from one end to the other linking what is taught from introduction of the unit to the concept, causes, effect, reason, etc. till the end of the unit.

What should be avoided in an explanation are irrelevant statements which do not contribute to the course of the content and can be done without.

Explanation is an intellectual activity which involves ideas, phenomenon, concepts etc. which are communicated to others (students) by giving examples, showing relationships, applying reasons, drawing inferences etc. Hence the skill has to be mastered. To acquire the skill of explaination the following components of the skill should be borne in mind, used and exposed while planning the unit.

- **Introductory statement:** It helps to draw the attention of the pupil towards the topic and also makes the pupil feel that he knows the topic and some of its contents. He gets interested in the unit and focuses his attention on what is going to be taught.
- **Clear voice, change in tone and pitch:** A clear voice makes the pupils want to listen carefully and the change in tone and pitch brings about a fluctuation in the content as to what is important and what other thing are present in its content. Quality of voice, its tone and pitch show emotions and attract pupils towards the content. It also breaks the monotony of an explanation
- **Continuous and fluent:** All explanations have to have a flow and be a continuation from one point to the next or even when linking one idea/ concept with the next. Language is a support for any explanation to be understood and this should contain proper words and sentences. The teacher has to be fluent.

- **Relevant to context:** All explanations made in a classroom should be such that it is based on the topic and helps to build the concept or theory of the unit taught. The matter covered during explanation should be relevant to the planned unit and help pupils focus, build and develop the unit.
- **Covering essential points.** The explanation should go with the planning of the unit and any support of examples or questions should be based on covering the essential points of the unit
- **Using explaining links:** Links used while teaching tells the pupils that the explanation is in progress. It helps in the flow of the unit and helps build the unit. At times it helps to stress on certain important part of the unit, or draw conclusions or in giving reason etc.
- **Simple relevant examples:** Examples help to clarify what is taught especially concepts, definitions etc. Examples also make the pupil feel as if he knows what is being taught since he is able to feel or understand the familiarity with the example.
- **Body movement and gestures:** The teacher moves from one place to another during the course of her teaching any lesson in a class. This maybe towards the chalk board to write some important point or draw the attention to something already on the board or towards a

student with a purpose like check the process or solution from his book or focus more on what he is answering. It captures the attention of the pupil and helps them to interact with the teacher for an answer or a solution or the correction of the process of working some solution. If the teacher is standing stiff in a place while explaining, it may not appeal to the students. It may become a mode for imitation of the teacher. Body movements help pupil to focus on the teacher, understand what she is teaching and what exactly she wants to say on the unit being taught. Gestures like pictures help students to get the concept and also break the monotony.

- **Made clear, using AV aids:** While explaining many a times use of the audio-visual aids help and support the teacher in clarifying and building the concept. This could be used in the school level in the explanation easily. (While teaching the unit, the student teacher should try to score on this component, by using av-aids to help her in the explanation of the unit.)
- **Used concluding statement:** All explanations come to an end using concluding statement. This could be done by recapitulation, or using questions or using charts etc. Concluding statements sum up the whole unit that is taught and help end the unit.

Name of Teacher (Teaching Class)						
S.No.	*Components*	*1*	*2*	*3*	*4*	*5*
1.	Introductory statement					
2.	Clear voice, change in tone and pitch					
3.	Continuous and fluent					
4.	Relevant to context					
5.	Covering essential points					
6.	Using explaining links					
7.	Simple relevant examples					
8.	Body movement and gestures					
9.	Made clear,using AV aids					
10.	Used concluding statement					
	Total					
Name of Teacher (Observing Class)						

3. Skill Audio-visual Aids

The use of audio-visual aid in the form of charts, models, diagrams, chemical reactions with apparatus, photos, pictures, live objects like leaves, flowers fish etc. makes any unit taught, interesting and the pupil are focused on the topic. But using the av-aid is also a technique and the mastery of this skill is essential for all teachers. It builds on the curiosity and interest of the students, to know more at a faster pace. All ages are interested to see and observe for themselves. Apart from this, the mind helps to build concepts and ideas about objects or persons simultaneously and helps in the understanding of the unit with enthusiasm. The selection of the av-aid and its relevancy at building the unit is very important. How the av-aid will help in the flow of the unit has to be borne in mind. Many units can be taught by this method. It also helps save time. To build this skill, focus on the following components should help build the skill in a teacher:

- **Clear, specific picture:** The audio-visual used should be clear sharp and about the topic being taught. It should help build the unit and understand the matter taught in class.
- **Size:** The size should be appropriate not too big or too small. It should help focus the attention of all the students. The subparts in the picture too should be proportionate and help in building the concept and understand the processes attached to the audio-visual.
- **Relevant to topic:** The audio-visual should be relevant and help in the unit building further. Huge pictures of authors rather than based on the content many a times become an irrelevant aid.. Audiovisual aids should be simple to help form concepts and ideas, based on the unit taught.
- **Stimulating:** Audio-visual aids if colourful, attractive and clear, or depending on the topic they happen to be funny, induce thinking, creativity and an interest in studying more from it. The audio-visual-aid. brings thoughts associated with the answer of the questions asked during the teaching or clarifies the understanding of the concept taught.
- **Creates interest and thinking:** The topic gets focused with the av aid and every student is

interested in studying the unit as well as knowing more about the unit. It makes thinking focused on the unit and helps further thinking

- **Helps understand unit:** The concepts of the unit are clear to understand and get linked to further parts of the unit. New ideas and the relations, causes and effect how and why get an answer due to the understanding becoming clear.
- **Seeking further information:** Students observing the picture, want to know more from the aid and also about the aid related to the unit taught. It pushes the thought processes to know more about the unit being taught to increase knowledge and further understanding.
- **Forms concept, idea, relationship:** The audio-visual-aid used should be showing the object clearly with proper size and should help the pupil understand what the teacher is teaching. The aid should help build the concept and also help further the topic. It should show the relationship of the topic with respect to size, parts, function, etc.
- **Students participation:** The eagerness to observe the av-aid will naturally stimulate the students to answer questions based on it in the class. It will also make them comment on the matter taught. They may even ask questions based on what they see in it. Hence the audio-visual - aid should be such that it brings such participation.
- **Assess students understanding:** Looking at the aid the teacher can ask questions to get the

students think with the help of the concrete object and answer with an understanding. Also the recapitulation can be done with the help of the audio-visual -aid. This can give an overall understanding of the unit taught.

Name of Teacher (Teaching Class)						
S.No.	*Components*	*1*	*2*	*3*	*4*	*5*
1.	Clear, specific picture					
2.	Size					
3.	Relevant to topic					
4.	Stimulating					
5.	Creates interest and thinking					
6.	Helps understand unit					
7.	Seeking further information					
8.	Forms concept, idea, relationship					
9.	Students participation					
10.	Assess students understanding					
	Total					
Name of Teacher (Observing Class)						

4. Skill Stimulus Variation

Whenever a teacher teaches a class he must know about the span of time that a student can focus on any activity, At the same time she cannot fix this span for all individuals as he has to keep in mind individual differences. On the other hand, he is bound by time and course of the subject to be completed. The attention of the child is bound to shift. Hence the teacher has to put in inputs which would focus the attention of the child as well as change the levels of sensory inputs.

The skill of stimulus variation implies attracting and focusing pupils attention by changing stimuli (using audio-visual aids, chalk board work, questioning etc.) in the environment of his study i.e. the class. For securing and sustaining pupils attention so that all the students are following what is taught with interest and understanding, the following components will help build the skill.

- **Body movements:** Lecturing can be boring. A teacher as an actor is something the children enjoy. She has to use her hands, neck, eyes and other parts of the body in course of his teaching to clarify her teaching. This variation in her body movements provide a brake from the monotonous class teaching and the student is paying attention to what is being taught by him in the classroom.
- **Gestures:** Keeping stiff is another boring act by the teacher for the student. A teacher who teaches doing actions, signals, motions, waves or nods is interacting with her students and they are responding to these gestures, every time they understand what is being taught..
- **Change in tone:** The fluctuation in the voice breaks the monotony in the explanation. Students seem to understand the emotions, character or say the severeness of the matter taught to them and pay attention. At times they seem to enjoy what is being said if there are fluctuations in the voice.

- **Pause:** While teaching brief periods of purposeful silence is used by the teacher to secure the attention of the pupil or to provide some short time for formulating the answer to a question asked in class or to check on if there is any doubt in the understanding of the concept or idea being taught.. Many times a teacher pauses in midway of his teaching, if some pupil is inattentive or disturbing in the class this focuses him to the unit under consideration. These pauses have to be used at appropriate places and they should not be too long or too short.
- **Teacher movement:** A teacher often moves in the class to check whether the student has any problem or he is doing the process correctly or asking questions. He also goes towards the blackboard to write something or point something relevant to what is being taught. This draws the attention of the child and keeps him focused to what is being taught. Aimless movements, wandering and pacing should be avoided as this distracts and irritates the pupils.
- **Audio-visual aids:** They help draw attention and focus the pupil to the matter taught in the class. They induce thinking, increase observation. It builds on the curiosity of the students and interest to know more at a faster pace. All children are interested to see and observe for themselves. Apart from this, the mind helps to build concepts and ideas about objects or persons and helps in

the understanding of the unit with enthusiasm, simultaneously. The monotone is broken.

- **Teacher-class interaction:** When the teacher teaches, he caters to the whole class. Many times she asks questions and almost all students respond to the question enthusiastically. The whole class is attentive and with what is being taught to the class. The students listen, understand and communicate it in this manner. Too much of it should be avoided to check noise, indiscipline etc. and hence this will call for a break in the type of stimulus.
- **Teacher-pupil interaction:** Here the teacher directs his attention to a particular pupil in terms of a nod or a question or by pointing the finger. The communication is between the teacher and a particular pupil who is supposed to respond. This focuses the attention of all the pupil and every one is paying attention and waiting for a chance to respond.
- **Focusing pupil's attention (verbal/gesture):** Here focusing refers to directing pupils attention to a particular point which they have to observe or understand. Statements like 'look at this picture', 'pay attention to what I am saying now', 'look at what happens when I do this' are all examples of verbal focusing. When gestures such as pointing, action, underlining etc are used the pupils pay attention to what is being taught and try to understand it.

- **Pupil movement-physical participation:** In this the student takes part in the activity or project or task assigned to the class. They may form groups for discussing and concluding, they may participate in solving on the board or drawing the diagram or labeling etc. All the students are involved and enjoy what is being taught.

Name of Teacher (Teaching Class)						
S.No.	*Components*	*1*	*2*	*3*	*4*	*5*
1.	Body movements					
2.	Gestures					
3.	Change in tone					
4.	Pause					
5.	Audio-visual aids					
6.	Teacher-class interaction					
7.	Teacher-pupil interaction					
8.	Focusing pupil's attention (verbal/gesture)					
9.	Pupil movement-physical participation.					
	Total					
Name of Teacher (Observing Class)						

5. Skill Reinforcement

It is a type of conditioning based on the feedback principle, which increases the individual to respond to similar situation as it gives a satisfaction to the individual self. Reinforcement promotes learning as the student is motivated to participate in the teaching in the class.

It helps to modify or decrease the undesirable behaviour, as a positive stimulus takes over the undesirable activity. It acts as an attention attracting device. An eagerness is seen in the pupils in class to answer to questions, wanting to know the correctness of the answer, waiting to show the progress of their class-works or even wanting to participate in any form of activity given by the teacher. Reinforcers are the types of feedback or responses that are got from the teacher which act as stimulants and change the whole environment of the class. A teacher should use these reinforcers and responses for themselves and responses to further the unit taught.

Reinforcement could be positive or negative. A positive reinforcer increases the probability of the response to recur in future whereas a negative reinforcer is any stimulus which makes the individual break that response (like a frown, punishment etc.). A teacher should use more of the positive reinforcement to encourage students to respond correctly, think for themselves and get the satisfaction of doing work in the class. Negative reinforcement like punishment, a loud 'No incorrect' are hard on the pupils and should be avoided as children are very sensitive and get demoralized immediately. Proper reinforcers have to be thus planned at various junctions by the teacher in his lesson. A planned lesson can yield the correct benefit of reinforcement as the answer and the timing of the reinforcers by the teacher is very important for a happy, understanding and progress of the lesson.

- **Positive verbal reinforcement:** Whenever a teacher teaches in the class, in the course of his teaching he asks questions or interacts with the pupil. The responses obtained from the students are encouraged by the teacher, by using terms such as 'good', 'that's right', 'well done' etc. Also words and phrases linking the answer like 'go on' 'continue', 'yes?' encourage pupils to participate and respond. Many times a sentence of praise at the good work, repetition of the students answer in the class while teaching, become positive verbal reinforcers.
- **Student deserved it:** Many a times the act of reinforcement becomes a habit (a mannerism) for the teacher in course of speaking. But it is important for the teacher to know the worth of the reinforcer and its impact on the student. Using them loosely all the time does not encourage the students from participating. At such times it could become a source of imitation of the teacher by the students and a joke. Hence it is important to use reinforcers so that they bring about a change in the students behaviour and encourage him to understand and participate.
- **Stimulating:** The encouragement that a student gets from his teacher makes him attentive, think and reason, respond, and participate in the classroom teaching. Therefore the reinforcers used should be able to do this. The student gets a positive feeling at paying attention, understanding

and listening to the questions asked. The repetition of the pupils answer or using it as a continuation in the teaching, acts as a stimulant for the pupils.

- **Providing lead/seeking further information.** The teacher uses certain answers from pupils to further his lesson. Sometimes certain reinforcers like a 'good', 'continue' 'what else' or 'similar examples?' act as a lead to further teaching. The student is stimulated to think and contribute on their own towards the progress of the unit taught. Hence the term 'providing lead/seeking further information'.
- **Positive non-verbal reinforcement:** Whenever a student is responding to what is taught, the teacher focuses on the student and encourages her by her eye contact, or by nodding her head, or giving an encouraging smile or a friendly look. The student wants to tell more and more of what he knows and pays attention to the activities in the class and the matter taught. The students are further encouraged and stimulated to participate in the unit and its activities in the class.
- **Writing pupils response on board:** The pupils answer or the important point he has made is noted many a times on the board. This gives the pupil a satisfaction and morally boosts him to pay attention and listen and think over the unit taught to him. A teacher may not realize this aspect but it is an important component which acts as a reinforcer..

- **Student's participation:** A lecture to the pupils is a boring process of passive listening by the pupils. Any class which is involved with the teacher is a better class and gives the proper vibrations to the teacher and encourages him to teach and deal with the unit in a democratic way. Student's participation not only stimulate the student to listen but also encourages the teachers to plan and develop the lesson so that there is an interactive progress of the unit.. Many a times it gives an evaluation of the unit understood by the class
- **Repetition of correct response was suitable:** It is found that whenever a correct response is given by the student, the teacher many a times repeats it. This encourages the student to respond to the unit taught in the class. But repeating the response in a meaningless manner or out of context can be discouraging to the student. Hence the correct timing and the proper answer has to be taken care of, by the teacher.
- **Wrong response weakened or broken:** The students are bound to give wrong answers at times. But it is important for the teacher to be careful how she deals with that student. Many times if she is not careful the child gets demoralized. Care should be taken to break the wrong answer subtly. There are many ways an efficient teacher can do this. Maybe one could be asking another student the answer to the same and if it is the correct one, asking the wrong answering

student to check the difference from his answer. The teacher could also ask an added question what made him contribute to the answer and slowly bring him to the correct answer and continue.

- **Teacher-pupil interaction:** In the past a silent class was preferred to any noise in the class. But today, the scenario has changed. A teacher has to have interactions with his pupils (by asking questions, stimulating them with situations and making them think and reply or organizing an activity). The pupil picks up the things taught more quickly and the understanding and reasoning on their own and answering gets a boost. The students enjoy learning and the teacher is motivated to teach systematically and in an organized manner, catering to all types of children in the class. Unnecessary noise of loose talk, irrelevant to what is being taught, should be avoided.

(*Contd...*)

Name of Teacher (Teaching Class)						
S.No.	*Components*	*1*	*2*	*3*	*4*	*5*
1.	Positive reinforcement(Good, Correct, Yes, Fine, Well done, Go on, Carry on, Go Ahead)					
2.	Student deserved					
3.	Stimulating					
4.	Providing lead/seeking further information					
5.	Positive non-verbal reinforcement (Nods, smiles, friendly look)					
6.	Writing pupils response on board					
7.	Students participation					
8.	Repetition of correct response was suitable					
9.	Wrong response weakened or broken					
10.	Teacher-pupil interaction					
	Total					
Name of Teacher (Observing Class)						

6. Skill Introduction of a lesson

Introduction is an important aspect in teaching as it helps to bring the students to focus and concentrate on the topic that is going to be taught now and at this moment. The teacher has to understand that the introduction brings to focus the presence of a teacher and the business she means to transact in the classroom. Introduction should be such that it makes the listener feel he knows the topic. He is eager to participate and pays full attention to what is being said. A good introduction, promises the listener of an interesting teaching-learning process ahead. Introducing a lesson to the class requires certain activities and organization on the part of the teacher and these are given in the form of components below. What best a teacher can do to achieve the components given below assures of a skillful introduction.

- **Greeting:** The teacher moves to the center of the class near the chalkboard, looks around the class, brings every child within her focus and greets the children a 'Good morning/afternoon etc...' The students simultaneously get ready to learn and put away the other activities they were involved in and focus on the teacher.
- **Previous knowledge suitable to level/ relevant to the topic:** Before coming to the topic, the teacher after understanding the topic and its contents, plans and selects to introduce the topic using some knowledge which the students already have, about some recent incident known to the class, some common sense theory or information that the students of that class have. This knowledge used by the teacher will lead to the topic and helps to focus the students to what is being told and also brings about their participation.
- **Gathering information from students:** When the teacher uses matter from the students to come to the topic, she is going to teach, she does this by questioning, listening to the answers, observing the interaction and participation of the students.
- **Enthusiastic response:** The students are eager to answer and involve themselves to the questions the

teacher asks them. They also contribute their views, thoughts and ideas from their past experiences based on the content. The teacher uses these before introducing the topic.

- **Students verbal/non-verbal involvement:** The response the students give the teacher may be verbal like answering the question or viewing their thoughts or the information they have or it may be non-verbal such as the attention they pay to the matter taught, nod their heads or smile or do some gestures in agreement or disagreement. Students even go to the extent of participating through the use of the chalk-board or showing some pictures they possess.
- **Interaction leading to topic:** The teacher uses the answers of the students and proceeds towards the topic. She may approach the topic with the help of what the students know, any novel idea they contribute and the points which form the part of the topic she will teach. This p0rocess makes the students feel they know the topic and this familiarity brings about an enthusiasm and eagerness in the students to learn more.
- **Focus on all students:** This is an important aspect of teaching because it works two ways – one the teacher is paying attention to all the students and two the students are focused on what she says and will say through her teaching process. The students are alert and concentrating and in turn it makes the teacher want to share more and more of the content in an easy and simple manner.

- **Positive and friendly expression:** The teachers' facial expressions play a key role in the responses and participation of the teacher-student interactions. A smiling and enthusiastic expression is an encouragement for the students to answer the teachers' questions. It helps to extend a warmth to the subject which is going to be taught.
- **Topic written on chalk board.** The whole introduction process gets focused on the topic. Writing the topic gives a clear-cut focus on what is going to be taught in the class. The topic on the board acts as a direction and also a process for the content to be taught. The teacher is focused as well as the students are focused on the classroom proceedings.
- **Used audio-visual aid.** They help draw attention and focus the pupil to the matter taught in the class. They induce thinking, increase observation. It builds on the curiosity of the students and interest to know more at a faster pace. All children are interested to see and observe for themselves. Apart from this, the mind helps to build concepts and ideas about objects or persons and helps in the understanding of the unit with enthusiasm, simultaneously. The monotone is broken, and the teacher is able to achieve the introduction to the topic more easily.

Introduction of a Lesson

S.No.	*Components of the skill*	*1*	*2*	*3*	*4*	*5*
1.	Greeting					
2.	Previous knowledge suitable to level/ relevant to the topic					
3.	Gathering information from students					
4.	Enthusiastic response					
5.	Students verbal/nonverbal involvement					
6.	Interaction leading to topic					
7.	Focus on all students					
8.	Positive and friendly expression					
9.	Topic written on chalk board					
10.	Used audio-visual aid					
	Total					
Total						

7. Skill: Achieving Closure

All explanations come to an end using concluding statement. This could be done by recapitulation, or using questions or using charts etc. Many times we just end topics abruptly taking it for granted that what is taught is understood perfectly well. This may not be the case all the time. A good teacher always uses concluding statements to sum up the whole unit that is taught and help end the unit.. It also acts as an indicator informing the teacher how well the unit is understood by the students. It helps students to reinforce the matter taught in the class and remember the content.

(1) Recap. Questions were sufficient: After completion of teaching the unit the teacher asks a number of questions based on the unit taught. This helps students to answer from the content understood during the class. It also helps teacher as it acts as a reinforcer to understand and know, how she has taught. A large no of questions, say about five or six on the important points from the unit taught has to be asked by the teacher. At times a teacher does not ask questions at the end or may ask just one question and wait for the answer. This does not help the teacher to know if the unit is understood neither does it inform the student the unit is over. Depending on the need, the no of questions need to be asked.

(2) Relevant questions: It should be relevant and based on the content that was taught. The questions asked are for recapitulation which makes you know whether the unit taught has formed the required concepts, and it is clear and understood well. In other words the questions help in determining the concept and the idea from the matter taught. Simultaneously the relationship in the contents or equations from the matter/statement of the content comes to the notice of the student as well as the teacher teaching the unit.

(3) Motivating questions: The question should hold the attention of the students, create an interest in answering what is known and understood. The question could even lead to think and apply the matter taught based on the question asked. As already said the questions should have quality rather than quantity and they should help the teacher teaching, assess the understanding of the unit by the students answers and make her know the level of the students understanding of the topic she has taught.

(4) **Students responding:** Questions should help in making the student involved in their thinking, exchanging and discussing the answers they give to the questions. They should not only be able to answer from the content taught but they should also be able to apply their own logic and reason to the questions.

(5) **Use of AV aids:** Audio-visual aids help and support the teacher in clarifying and building the concepts she has decided to build in the minds of the pupils. In recapitulation the teacher can easily use the AV aid in the form of chart, model, diagram etc, as a tool to end her lesson and simultaneously understand how much the student has understood. The eagerness to observe the av-aid will naturally stimulate the students to answer questions based on it. Asking questions on the unit and keeping the aid displayed increases the interactions and enthusiasm of the students. The teacher may ask students to point the relevant part of the question or they may draw a particular part or identify the answer from the aid. These are

some ways to know whether the student has understood the unit towards the end of the class. Thus she is able to achieve closure of the unit. It also helps to assess students overall understanding of the unit taught.

(6) **Use of Black Board:** During her teaching the teacher must organise the BB in such a way that everything that is taught is systematically arranged on the board. It may be in the form of points, diagram, words or sentences. After coming to the end of the unit, the teacher asks a few questions or gives some motivating task/ H.W. for the student to do and come the next day Using the matter written on the board is a technique which can act as a reinforcer and involve the students participation easily while recapitulating. Asking questions based on the matter on the board, making students come and underline the point answered on the board or reading the answer from the board could be some ways of using the BB. The teacher may also ask the student to draw, write or calculate some class task, which will show her that the students are following her.

(7) **Used Reinforcement/ Writing/ Underlining or ticking on Black Board:** At the end of teaching the teacher asks the pupils to answer some questions or suggest some applications of the matter taught. She may even note the important point made by the student onto the board. This gives the pupil a satisfaction and

morally boosts him to pay attention and listen and think over the unit taught to him and study further on the topic. A teacher may not realize this aspect but it is an important component which acts as a reinforcer.

(8) **Expressions friendly:** A friendly expression on the teachers face, adds warmth to whatever is taught by her to the students. The students feel comfortable to participate or answer to any thing asked of them. A smile, a 'yes' or a 'no' verbally or nonverbally, an eye contact, an expression on the face of asking or not knowing or encouragement are welcomed by all, unlike a stern or a tensed expression. A friendly expression motivates a student to be involved in the proceedings of the class.

(9) **Students know the unit is over:** The teacher has asked sufficient questions on whatever she has taught. She has reinforced the answers and also conveyed that the students have understood well. She may even give them some simple tasks as assignment which maybe something to think about or think over. It may be to calculate or to find out similar applications . The teacher may even say 'good class', 'thank you', 'read and come tomorrow' or ' we shall discuss……. tomorrow'

(10) **Easy assignments given:** A teacher is utilizing the attention and energy of the student for all the time she spends with them in the class. She should bear this in mind as well as remember that the next teacher who comes to the class will also be expecting

the same from the child. Hence whenever tasks are given they should be simple and motivating as well as achievable. Giving task for the sake of a routine can do no good to anybody. She should give them easy achievable task which she is going to follow up the next time. The same eagerness and wanting to learn should be reflected in the task given.

Achieving Closure

S.No.	*Components of the skill*	*1*	*2*	*3*	*4*	*5*
1.	Recap. Questions were sufficient					
2.	Relevant questions					
3.	Motivating questions					
4.	Students responding					
5.	Use of AV aids					
6.	Use of Black Board					
7.	Used Reinforcement/ Writing or ticking on BB					
8.	Expressions friendly					
9.	Students know the unit is over					
10.	Easy assignments given					
	Total					
Total						

8. Skill Response Management

Today we have to acknowledge the mental level of the students. The teacher cannot use the lecture method to transact the matter she has decided to teach, in the class. The student knows more and is better aware of things happening around. Hence while teaching, a smart and conscious teacher will teach involving the students in her classroom transaction. For this, she encourages participation and interaction from the students. Questions, suggestion, comments and discussions are monitored by the teacher. The teacher tries to get from the students what they know and puts forward from her side what they do not know. This is an effective process, not only for the students who know, but it is more interesting even for the students who do not know. This skill includes responses which are to be obtained from the pupils by the teacher. The teacher uses verbal and non-verbal stimulants in the form of questions, suggestions or an expression which makes the pupil think and contribute the answer. Thus, the students are involved in the teaching-learning process. Pupils on their part are motivated to think, reason, answer, participate, give their own knowledgeable direction and be with what the teacher is teaching. They feel they are forwarding the unit rather than the teacher who is managing the responses, through this skill.

(1) **Motivating questions:** The question should hold the attention of the students, create an interest in knowing and understanding the question, thereby leading to think on the question asked, and draw an answer. As already said the questions should have quality rather than quantity and they should help the teacher teaching, assess the understanding of the unit by the students' answers and make him know the level of the students understanding of the topic he has taught.

(2) **Questions short & easily understood:** It should be specific and straight to find what the particular answer is. It should be relevant and based on the content being taught. The language used to ask the question should be easy. It should be short. Long 'breathless' questions should be avoided. The idea behind the question should be to know what the student knows, involve him in your class and keep him motivated in the classroom transactions. Questions should yield the answers that will help forward progress of the unit taught.

(3) **Prompting/cues/hints:** Many times when the students are asked questions they are unable to answer, or may be confused or the question may have more than one answer. When such a question is asked the teacher has to take care of all the answers. Many times passing the question to other students may send a wrong message to the student in the form of 'I am unable to answer', 'I don't understand at all' or 'I am a weak student' which might lead to a mental block in the child. Hence a teacher should use prompting or giving cues to the student to answer the question.The question can be broken into smaller units or sub-questions and then asked. The teacher can hint or ask small questions leading to the correct answer.

(4) **Seeking information/thought/idea:** The questions asked should be such that the students'

think and want to know ahead of the contents of the lesson and the question has provoked them to go ahead in the sequence of their thought. This stimulation makes them think and know more about the contents.

(5) **Re-focusing:** This is a technique used where the responses obtained are further applied to similar and different aspects of the question asked. When a student answers a question, she is asked further questions on similar cases and the concept cleared. The teacher can also use different objects, models to ask about the commonness and differences on these objects.Thus the pupil is stimulated to think about the similarities and dissimilarities of the related facts and situation and build up on his understanding process.

(6) **Re-directing:** This technique motivates the students to participate and involve himself with the teachers flow of teaching. Re-direction is mostly used when the student does not answer or when the answer is an inaccurate answer. The teacher then directs the question to another student. Many times one question may have more than one response. In such cases too the teacher acknowledges the answer and directs the question to other students. Re-direction can also be used to reinforce an answer and build on the concept.

(7) **Questions stimulate to think beyond:** The question should hold the attention of the students, create an interest in knowing and

understanding the question, thereby leading to think on the question asked and draw an answer. The encouragement that a student gets from his teacher makes him attentive, think and reason, respond, and participate in the classroom teaching. Therefore the reinforcers used should be able to do this. The student gets a positive feeling at paying attention, understanding and listening to the questions asked. The repetition of the pupils answer or using it as a continuation in the teaching, acts as a stimulant for the pupils. The student is thus encouraged to think more and also beyond the question asked.

(8) **Students focused :** The students are focused in the class depending on various factors like the teacher makes the lesson interesting, there are models and charts for them to observe and understand, there is a lot of stimulation from the teacher, the student is encouraged to think and reason. No student feels demoralized or low at voicing their thoughts. The teachers focus is on every child. She asks or speaks to every child. The students concentration is on what is being taught by the teacher and he is very focused . This is an important aspect of teaching because it works two ways – one the teacher is paying attention to all the students and two the students are focused on what she says and will say through her teaching process.

(9) **Reinforcement**. Reinforcement promotes learning as the student is motivated to participate

in the teaching in the class. It helps to modify or decrease the undesirable behaviour, as a positive stimulus takes over the undesirable activity. It acts as an attention attracting device. An eagerness is seen in the pupils in class to answer to questions, wanting to know the correctness of the answer, waiting to show the progress of their class-works or even wanting to participate in any form of activity given by the teacher. Reinforcers are the types of feedback or responses that are got from the teacher which act as stimulants and change the whole environment of the class. A teacher should use these reinforcers and see for themselves the response of the class towards the unit taught.

Reinforcement could be positive or negative. A positive reinforcer increases the probability of the response to recur in future whereas a negative reinforcer is any stimulus which makes the individual break that response (like a frown, punishment etc.). A teacher should use more of the positive reinforcement to encourage students to respond correctly, think for themselves and get the satisfaction of doing work in the class. Negative reinforcement like punishment, a loud 'No incorrect' are hard on the pupils and so should be avoided as children are very sensitive and get demoralized immediately. Proper reinforcers have to be thus planned at various junctions by the teacher in her lesson. A planned lesson can yield the correct benefit of reinforcement as the answer and the timing of the reinforcers by the teacher is very important for a happy, understanding and progress of the lesson. The pupils answer or the important point he has made is noted many a times on the board. This gives the pupil a satisfaction and morally boosts him to pay attention and listen and think over the unit taught to him. A teacher may not realize this aspect but it is an important component which acts as a reinforcer.

(10) **Classroom control:** This comes with the teachers command over the topic she is going to teach. The planning and preparation for the classroom transaction is automatically transferred to the student. The student is thus attentive and wants to learn. The teacher too has to involve the student in her class by questioning, asking them to write on the board or books, taking a round in the class, observing the students and having them in her focus.

Skill Response Management

S.No.	*Components of the skill*	*1*	*2*	*3*	*4*	*5*
1.	Motivating questions					
2.	Questions short & easily understood					
3.	Prompting/cues/hints					
4.	Seeking information/ thought/idea					
5.	Re-focusing					
6.	Re-directing					
7.	Questions stimulate to think beyond					
8.	Students focused					
9.	Reinforcement					
10.	Classroom control					
	Total					
Total						

9. Skill: Illustrating with Examples

It is an age old method where we find the older generation resorting to examples to drive their point. In teaching a lot of explanation is involved. Just explanation can be monotonous and at times, not easily understood. Using examples clarifies the concept, theme or theory under consideration. Examples act as an illustration of that thought and make the abstract idea or mathematical explanation/concept of the content easy to understand. It helps to build the unit further.

If examples are from the pupils daily life and used within the teaching, it makes the content familiar and known. They motivate and stimulate the listener and draw their attention. Hence it becomes easy to assimilate. Examples need not only be in the form of explanation but there could be visual examples in the form of models, charts, diagrams etc. they could even be in the form of auditory example or tactual example. Auditory in the form of related stories, events, imitation etc, and tactual meaning should be by using real or actual objects.

(1) **Relevant examples:** When examples are used they should try to help build the concept, idea or theme and clarify what is to be taught by the teacher. They should bring about the similarities or differences analogous to the content taught. The examples used to cover the content during explanation should be relevant to the planned unit and help pupils focus, build and develop the unit.

(2) **Clears concept/content taught:** The example used helps in determining the concept and the idea from the matter taught. Simultaneously the relationship of the contents or equations from the matter/statement of the content is easily linked to the example and the student is able to understand the concept/content to be taught.

(3) **Simple and easy:** Examples help to clarify what is taught especially concepts, definitions etc. Examples also make the pupil feel as if he knows what is being taught since he is able to feel or

understand the familiarity with the example. These examples should be simple and the language used should be even more simple and easy to understand.

(4) **Student interaction:** The eagerness, with which students understand the example, stimulates the students to answer questions and participate in the class. It also makes them interact and be an active participant, as the example helps to build a familiarity to the content taught.

(5) **Seeks further information:** Students listening to the example try to correlate it to the subject taught and want to know more, related to the unit taught. It pushes the thought processes towards the unit being taught and tries to increase the knowledge and helps further understanding.

(6) **Correlates with the topic:** Whenever examples are used they should be linked to what we want to correlate in the form of similarity or difference with respect to the content. They should not be used for the sake of using or because you feel you know one example and the skill to be used is 'Illustrating with examples'.

(7) **Used as a lead:** The teacher uses certain examples to further his lesson. Sometimes certain familiar/similar examples act as a lead to further teaching. The student is stimulated to think and contribute on their own towards the progress of the unit taught.

(8) **Question/explanation with respect to topic content clarity:** The teacher uses the example to teach the unit but many times it may not be clear. The teacher then asks questions or gives explanation correlating it to the example. Thus she achieves a clear concept of the unit taught, at the same time students also think and realise the relevance of the example.

Skill Illustrating with examples:

S.No.	*Components of the skill*	*1*	*2*	*3*	*4*	*5*
1.	Relevant examples					
2.	Clears concept/content taught					
3.	Simple and easy					
4.	Student interaction					
5.	Seeksfurther information					
6.	Correlates with the topic					
7.	Used as a lead					
8.	Question/explanation w.r.t. topic content clarity					
	Total					
Total						

10. Skill Narration

This skill is used more at the primary level in schools. Narration involves describing and giving details of stories, incidents or events. Narration can be both oral and written. We shall only deal with the **oral use in classroom** by the teacher. (Written could be written by teacher and analysed by students or it could be written by students and analysed by teacher.) This skill makes the teacher use her voice and embed the flow of her thoughts into the minds of the students. The teacher is able to take along the students mentally into the story or event she narrates. The language she uses, the gestures and facial expressions that go with the narration helps to create interest and enthusiasm to know more of what she speaks of the event. The student develops the concept and understanding of the unit. Many a times the student is also able to feel and be a part of the narrated unit.

(1) **Simple language according to level:** The language used should be simple and easy to understand. It should suit the level of the child. Simple vocabulary with simpler phrases and idioms should be used. Short sentences and easy flowing language should be used. A higher set of vocabulary words and build up of sentences are suitable to grownup children of higher classes.

(2) **Voice modulation (pitch/tone):** The fluctuation in the voice breaks the monotony in the explanation and teaching. Students seem to understand the emotions, character or say the seriousness in the matter taught to them and pay attention. At times they seem to enjoy what is being said with fluctuations in the voice.

(3) **Gestures and facial expressions:** Keeping stiff is another boring act by the teacher for the

student. A teacher who narrates to teach, doing actions, signals, motions, waves, nods or enacts is interacting with her students and they are responding to these gestures, every time and they understand what is being taught. Gestures may be used to indicate size, shape, idea of movement, or any action. The teacher may even move from one point to another during the course of her narrating any lesson in a class. This maybe near the chalk board or her table which acts as an attention drawing act, It captures the attention of the pupil and helps them to interact with the teacher. If the teacher is standing stiff in a place while narrating, it may not appeal that well, to the students. It may becomes a mode for imitation of the teacher. Body and facial movements help pupil to focus on the teacher, understand what she is teaching and what exactly she wants to say on the unit being taught. Gestures like pictures help students to get the concept and also break the monotony.

(4) **Changes the form of speech:** The narrator uses both direct and indirect speech during the course of his teaching. Direct speech is better used for depicting what a character said along with the voice modulation and stress on the dialogue. Students get a better picture and concept of how things happened in the presence of all characters even though it is the same teacher modifying her voice. Indirect

speech could be used to explain the story with, in between add-ons of direct speech.

(5) **Language appropriate to situation:** Short sentences and easy flowing language should be used. It should be sharp and related to the situation so that it makes students understand the situation narrated in a clear manner,

(6) **Continuity in narrative:** Whenever the skill of narration is used, there are incidents or events involved. The teacher should be clear in the sequence of the events, when it occurred and what the next event was and so on, so that the student gets a clear picture of the different situation, their occurrence and the details of the event. In addition, the skill also emphasizes, how the teacher is able to link the different events to narrate the whole story or event as a continuous and interesting occurrence of events.

(7) **Regular focus on students:** When a teacher narrates, she must look at the students and not just read and narrate or look anywhere other than the students. She must have the eye contact with the class as a whole and also understand the expressions on the face of the students. This helps the teacher to understand the students are paying attention, they are interested and are with your narration or not.

(8) **Speed of narrative:** Depending on the event, the character and the situation in the narration

the speed of the narrative has to be modified. It depends on the teacher how she modifies the speed of the narrative to maintain the logic, sequence on one hand and the interest and richness of the narration on the other hand.

(9) **Correct pronunciation:** Correct pronunciation fixes and remains in the minds of the students. We Indians can have a variety of accents belonging to the different states but the pronunciation has to be accurate as it will give the correct meaning to the sentence. We should also remember that pronunciation when tagged with voice modulation and pause at the right juncture, leads to very effective narration.

(10) **Fluency:** All narrations have to have a flow and be continuous from one point to the next, from one event to the next or even when linking one idea/concept with the next. Language acts as a support for any narration and does the explanation to be understood and this should contain proper words and sentences and the teacher has to be fluent.

(*Contd...*)

Skill Narration:

S.No.	*Components of the skill*	*1*	*2*	*3*	*4*	*5*
1.	Simple language according to level					
2.	Voice modulation (pitch/tone)					
3.	Gestures and facial expressions					
4.	Changes the form of speech					
5.	Language appropriate to situation					
6.	Continuity in narrative					
7.	Regular focus on students					
8.	Speed of narrative					
9.	Correct pronunciation					
10.	Fluency					
	Total					
Total						

11. Skill: Recitation

This skill is also mostly used at the elementary level. This skill makes use of the delivery of poems, passages, quotations mostly memorizing them and repeating loudly, clearly and without changing the content or idea. The reciter (in this case the teacher) has to repeat the passage putting in the feelings and emotions of the writer or poet and conveys to them aloud what they want to say in the particular poem or passage.

(1) **Clarity of voice:** A clear voice makes the pupils want to listen carefully and **the** change in tone

and pitch brings about a fluctuation in the content as to what is important and what other thing are present in its content. Quality of voice, its tone and pitch show emotions and attract pupils towards the content. It also breaks the monotony of recitation.

(2) **Correct pronunciation:** Correct pronunciation fixes and remains in the minds of the students. We Indians can have a variety of accents belonging to the different states but the pronunciation has to be accurate as it will give the correct meaning to the sentences in the recited para. We should also remember that pronunciation when tagged with voice modulation and pause, at the right juncture leads to very effective recitation.

(3) **Rhythm, accent:** Prose or poetry, every content has a rhythm of its own. The teacher uses the words and phrase she recites and makes the words flow with a certain musical quality. This particular manner of bringing rhythm into the passage is the teachers own style. It has feelings and emotions which will give the theme within the recitation. The students too find it easier to remember the content along with the rhythm attached to it.

(4) **Gesture & facial expression:** Keeping stiff is another boring act by the teacher seen by the student. A teacher who recites using certain actions ,signals, motions, waves, nods or enacts

is interacting with her students and they are responding to these gestures, every time and they understand what is being taught. Gestures may be used to indicate size, shape, idea of movement, or any action. The teacher may even move from one point to another during the course of her recitation. It captures the attention of the pupil and helps them to interact with the teacher. Body and facial movements help pupil to focus on the teacher, understand what he is teaching through the recitation and understand what exactly he wants to say about the unit being taught. Gestures like pictures help students to get the concept and also break the monotony.

(5) **Speed:** Depending on the event, the character and the situation in the poem, the passage recited and the speed of the recitation has to be modified. It depends on the teacher how she modifies the speed, to maintain the logic, sequence on one hand and the interest and richness of the recitation on the other.

(6) **Fluency:** All recitations have to have a flow and be continuous from one point to the next, from one event to the next or even when linking one idea/concept with the next. Language and rhythm acts as a support for any recitation and does the explanation to be understood and this should contain properly pronounced words and sentences. Hence, the teacher has to be fluent.

(7) **Focus on students:** When a teacher recites, she must look at the students and not read or narrate or look anywhere other than the students. She must have the eye contact with the class as a whole and also understand the expressions on the face of the students. This helps the teacher to understand that the students are paying attention, they are interested and are with her recitation or not.

(8) **Students attentive**: When reciting, many a times the teacher is in her own world of recitation. Monotonous, hasty, rhythm-less recitation may force students to be inattentive. No eye contact or focus on students may make students comment, imitate or get distracted to other activities.

Skill Recitation:

S.No.	*Components of the skill*	*1*	*2*	*3*	*4*	*5*
1.	Clarity of voice					
2.	Correct pronunciation					
3.	Rhythm, accent					
4.	Gesture &facial expression					
5.	Speed					
6.	Fluency					
7.	Focus on students					
8.	Students attentive					
	Total					
Total						

12. Skill: Pupil Participation/Interaction

Today we have to acknowledge the mental level of the students. The teacher cannot use the lecture method to transact the matter she has decided to, to the class. The student knows more and is better aware of things happening around. Hence while teaching, a smart and conscious teacher will teach involving the students in her classroom transaction. Participation and interaction are not only for the students who know but it is an effective process even for the students who do not know. This skill includes activities on the part of the pupils and teacher both. The teacher uses verbal and non-verbal stimulants to involve students in the teaching-learning process. Pupils on their part are motivated to think, reason, answer, participate, give their own knowledgeable direction and be with what the teacher is teaching.

(1) **Lower order question:** The teacher asks simple questions from what the students know and creates an easy atmosphere in the class. She builds her unit beginning with what the students know.

(2) **Higher order questions:** The questions here are of the type which makes the pupil think, analyse and reason. The student probes his memory with respect to the content and is involved in understanding the unit and answering these questions. Even if the student gives a wrong answer, the teacher encourages the student by correcting these answers in a subtle and easy manner so that the wrong answer is erased and the correct answer has replaced it.

(3) **Long answer question:** Long here means more than a single sentence. Some students are made to participate using such questions and contributing their thoughts by such participation.

(4) **Open ended question:** These questions have more than one answer and more students are involved answering them. These questions are thought provoking and many pupils have experienced more than one aspect of the answer.

(5) **Prompting:** Many times when the students are asked questions they are unable to answer, or may be confused or the question may have more than one answer. When such a question is asked the teacher has to take care that passing the question to other students, may send a wrong message to the student in the form of 'I am unable to answer', 'I don't understand at all' or 'I am a weak student' which might lead to a mental block in the child. Hence a teacher should use prompting or giving cues to the student to answer the question.The question can be broken into smaller units or sub-questions and then asked. The teacher can hint or ask small questions leading to the correct answer.

(6) **Redirected question:** This technique motivates the students to participate and involve himself with the teachers flow of teaching. Re-direction is mostly used, when the student does not answer or when the answer is an inaccurate answer. The teacher then directs the question to another

student. Many times one question may have more than one response. In such cases too the teacher directs the question to other students. Re-direction can also be used to reinforce an answer and build on the concept.

(7) **Reinforcement positive (verbal and non-verbal):** Reinforcement promotes learning as the student is motivated to participate in the teaching in the class. It helps to modify or decrease the undesirable behaviour, as a positive stimulus takes over the undesirable activity. It acts as an attention attracting device. An eagerness is seen in the pupils in class, to answer questions, wanting to know the correctness of the answer, waiting to show the progress of their class-works or even wanting to participate in any form of activity, given by the teacher. Reinforcers are the types of feedback or responses that are got from the teacher which act as stimulants and change the whole environment of the class. A teacher should use these reinforcers and see for themselves the response of the class towards the unit taught.

Reinforcement could be positive or negative. A positive reinforcer increases the probability of the response to recur in future whereas a negative reinforcer is any stimulus which makes the individual break that response (like a frown, punishment etc.). A teacher should use more of the positive reinforcement to encourage students to respond correctly, think for themselves and get the satisfaction of doing work in the class. Negative reinforcement like punishment, a loud 'No incorrect' is hard on the pupils and so should be avoided as children are very sensitive and get demoralized immediately. Proper reinforcers have to be thus planned at various junctions by the teacher in her lesson . A planned lesson can yield the correct benefit of reinforcement as the answer and the timing of the reinforcers by the teacher is very important for a happy, understanding and progress of the lesson. The pupils answer or the important point he has made is noted many a times on the board. This gives the pupil a satisfaction and morally boosts him to pay attention and listen and think over the unit taught to him. A teacher may not realize this aspect but it is an important component which acts as a reinforcer.

(8) **Using answers as lead:** The questions asked (or thoughts expressed) by the students should be such that the students are thinking and wanting to know ahead of the contents of the lesson. The question has to provoke them to go ahead in the sequence of their thought and stimulate them to think and know more about the contents.

(9) **Pupils physical participation:** The Pupil is asked to draw, write or point out on the board. He may even be asked to use himself as a model and explain the answer to the question asked. Many a times the student is asked to show the

parts or explain with the help of the model or chart present in the class.

(10) **Movement & pause**: The teacher moves in the class which makes the student aware of her presence and he is attentive in the class. A teacher often moves in the class to check whether the student has any problem or he is doing the process correctly or asking questions. She also goes towards the blackboard to write something or point something relevant to what is being taught. This draws the attention of the child and keeps him focused to what is being taught. Aimless movements, wandering and pacing should be avoided as this distracts and irritates the pupils. While teaching brief periods of purposeful silence is used by the teacher to secure the attention of the pupil or to provide some short time for formulating the answer to a question asked in class or to check on, if there is any doubt in the understanding of the concept or idea being taught.. Many times a teacher pauses midway of his teaching. If some pupil is inattentive or disturbing in the class it focuses him to the unit under consideration. These pauses have to be used at appropriate places and they should not be too long or too short.

(11) **Involved all Pupils:** When the teacher teaches, he caters to the whole class. Many times he asks questions and almost all students respond to the question enthusiastically. The whole class is

attentive to what is being taught to the class. The students listen, understand and communicate it in this manner. Too much of it should be avoided to check noise, indiscipline etc. and hence it calls for a break in the type of stimulus. At times the teacher directs his attention to a particular pupil in terms of a nod or a question or by pointing the finger. The communication is between the teacher and a particular pupil who is supposed to respond. This focuses the attention of all the pupil and every one is paying attention and waiting for a chance to respond

SkillPupil Participation/Interaction

S.No.	*Components of the skill*	*1*	*2*	*3*	*4*	*5*
1.	Lower order question					
2.	Higher order question					
3.	Long answer question					
4.	Open ended question					
5.	Prompting					
6.	Redirected question					
7.	Reinforcement positive (verbal and non-verbal)					
8.	Using answers as lead					
9.	Pupils physical participation					
10.	Movement & pause					
11.	Involved all pupils					
	Total					
Total						

13. Skill: Dramatization

When we use this skill, we are actually enacting, replicating or role playing the contents given to characters in the content. It is a stimulating skill which not only focuses the students to the content but also it adds entertainment to the teaching-learning process.

(1) **Situation/unit requires it:** Many units can be covered by this skill. But certain units become effective and come alive with this skill. There are dialogues, voice modulations, role requirement which makes dramatization a necessary skill to understand the unit.

(2) **Relevant dialogues used:** The dialogues are meaningful and lead to understanding the situation and the role of the character. They are rendered in the required tone of the voice and part of the unit. They help in promoting the content of the unit.

(3) **Conversational language used:** The dialogues are understood and are simple and easy to understand. It is of the level of the students. They bring alive the character in the unit.

(4) **Correct pronunciation:** Correct pronunciation fixes and remains in the minds of the students. We Indians can have a variety of accents belonging to the different states but the pronunciation has to be accurate as it will give the correct meaning to the sentences in the spoken dialogues. We should also remember that pronunciation when tagged with clear-cut voice,

voice modulation and pause, at the right juncture leads to very effective rendering of dialogues in dramatisation.

(5) **Identification with role:** The teacher using this skill should mould with the role and identify with it. Even if it means adding a scarf or a crown or any external material to give an emphasis on the role enacted. The facial expressions, voice, actions should match the role.

(6) **Student participation:**The student knows more and is better aware of things happening around. Hence while teaching, using the dramatisation skill, a smart and conscious teacher will enact and teach, involving the students in her classroom transaction. Participation and interaction as part of the character are not only for the students who know but it is an effective process even for the students who do not know. This skill includes activities on the part of the pupils and teacher both. If the teacher does not include the students in the role then she may use means of knowing whether the students have understood the roles and its importance. This may be done by brief questions or discussion. Hence, the teacher uses verbal and non-verbal stimulants to encourage and involve students in the teaching-learning process. Pupils on their part are motivated to think, reason, answer, participate, and understand the unit and the importance of the role and dialogues used by the teacher.

(7) **Student understand situation:** The unit taught by this skill, makes the student understand the background, situation and the importance of the role. He is made to think and motivated to be part of the drama. He understands the why's, how's and the timing of the situation by the proper dramatisation of the situation.

(8) **Student conscious of the role requirement:** The student knows and understands the requirement of the role. He understands why the voice was loud, why it was soft or why it was cracking. He is able to appreciate the character played by the teacher and through it he understands the real situation of the unit written by the unit's author.

(9) **Voice & gestures appropriate:** A clear voice makes the pupils want to listen carefully and the change in tone and pitch brings about a fluctuation in the content as to what is important and what other things are present in its content. Quality of voice, its tone and pitch show emotions and attract pupils towards the content. It also breaks the monotony of speech. A teacher who dramatises using certain actions, signals, motions, waves, nods or enacts is interacting with her students and they are responding to these gestures, every time and they understand what is being taught. Gestures may be used to indicate size, shape, idea of movement, or any action. The teacher may even move from one point to another during the course of her

recitation. It captures the attention of the pupil and helps them to interact with the teacher. Body and facial movements help pupil to focus on the teacher, understand what he is teaching through the actions and know exactly he wants to say teaching the unit. Gestures, just like pictures help students to get the concept and also break the monotony.

(10) Act clarifies the theme/content: This part has to e borne in the minds of the teacher dramatizing the unit. The ultimate aim of the skill is to make pupils understand the unit with its background and situation and how it could be, as depicted by dramatizing it. Thus this clarification can be obtained by asking the students, questions on the unit dramatized. Their views and opinions may even at times give a thought or view which we will have to think about and understand the situation of the unit.

(*Contd...*)

Skill Dramatization

S.No.	*Components of the skill*	*1*	*2*	*3*	*4*	*5*
1.	Situation/unit requires it					
2.	Relevant dialogues used					
3.	Conversational language used					
4.	Correct pronunciation					
5.	Identification with role					
6.	Student participation					
7.	Student understand situation					
8.	Student conscious of the role requirement					
9.	Voice & gestures appropriate					
10.	Act clarifies the theme/content					
	Total					
Total						

14. Skill: Classroom Management:

The whole perspective of teaching –learning has changed. For a good teacher classroom management comes easily. This concept "GOOD" means, a teacher who is skillful, well versed with her subject, keeps herself abreast with new knowledge, acknowledges students thoughts and ideas and appreciates her students abilities and knowledge of the subject. A teacher has to attend to each and every student in the class. Classrooms today, contain gifted and backward students too. Depending on how the teacher tackles and reaches out to the student will determine her classroom management. Classroom management does not mean a quiet class but it means a vibrant attentive class, ready to think reason and apply their minds to what is being taught.

(1) **Pupils in focus/view of teacher:** When a teacher teaches, she must look at the students and not read or narrate or look anywhere other than the students. She must have the eye contact with the class as a whole and also understand the expressions on the face of the students. This helps the teacher to understand the students are paying attention, they are interested and are with her teaching or not.

(2) **Instructs students on expected behaviour in classroom:** A teacher should encourage students to answer and voice their opinions about the content when she asks them to. A chorus answer will lead to indiscipline hence she should instruct them to raise their hands when they want to answer or speak. A teacher should subtly tell the students she does not want unnecessary talking or noise in her class.

(3) **Explains and has eye contact with students:** When a teacher explains, she must look at the students and have the eye contact with the class as a whole and also understand the expressions on the face of the students. She must respond to these expressions and make the pupil feel she understands, he is having a problem or this part is interesting etc. This also helps the teacher to

understand the students are paying attention, they are interested and are with her during the course of teaching.

(4) **Commanding voice/flexible for appreciation & dislike:** The teacher has a commanding voice which makes the student pay attention to the teachings in the class. This voice is not monotonous but changes according to the needs of the content and response of the students. At times she is soft and encouraging, at times she is smiling and appreciating the students' reactions

(5) **Ensures sufficient work for pupils:** When the teacher is teaching the students are paying attention but when the teacher is not teaching the students are busy with some work like sums or thinking of means to achieve a soln or planning an activity or so on. They are not left to chit-chat, roam about or be indisciplined.

(6) **Reinforces attentive behaviour:** Reinforcement promotes learning as the student is motivated to participate and be attentive to the teaching in the class. It helps to modify or decrease the undesirable behaviour, as a positive stimulus takes over the undesirable activity. It acts as an attention attracting device. An eagerness is seen in the pupils in class to answer to questions, wanting to know the correctness of the answer, waiting to show the progress of their class-works or even wanting to participate in any form of activity given by the teacher. Reinforcers are the types of

feedback or responses that are got from the teacher which act as stimulants and change the whole environment of the class. A teacher should use these reinforcers and see for herself the response of the class towards the unit taught.

(7) **Questions in all direction:** Questions asked at different intervals in the class, prevents students from diverting their attention from the teacher and her teaching. The students await their turn to be questioned and listen carefully to the classroom activity. The focus is on the teacher and there is minimum distraction in the class.

(8) **Students interact appropriately:** The student knows more and is better aware of things happening around. .When the teacher teaches, she caters to the whole class. Many times she asks questions and almost all students respond to the question enthusiastically. This shows that the whole class is attentive. The students listen, understand and communicate it in this manner. Too much of it should be avoided to check noise, indiscipline etc. and hence this will call for a break in the type of stimulus. At times the teacher directs her attention to a particular pupil in terms of a nod or a question or by pointing the finger. The communication is between the teacher and a particular pupil who is supposed to respond. This focuses the attention of all the pupil and every one is paying attention and waiting for a chance to respond. Checking over-

enthusiasm to answer, in a chorus, will ensure discipline in the class.

(9) **Chit-chat/noise controlled:** The teacher should instruct the students in the beginning itself that they should not unnecessarily chit-chat in the class. At times she should question the student 'chit-chatting', on the unit being taught. She can even make signs or verbally tell them to stop it, because others are missing out on what is being taught.

(10) **Management of time:** The teacher has to plan how much time and how much content can be transacted in that time.All the components planned for teaching the unit should fit in the time period. If it does not then it is better to take a smaller unit rather than going on teaching. Remember in a microteaching class, we are developing our skills rather than trying to make our colleagues (who are students) intelligent and knowledgeable about the content.

(*Contd...*)

Skill Classroom Management

S.No.	*Components of the skill*	*1*	*2*	*3*	*4*	*5*
1.	Pupils in focus/view of teacher					
2.	Instructs students expected behaviour in classroom					
3.	Explains & has eye contact with students					
4.	Commanding voice/flexible for appreciation & dislike					
5.	Ensures sufficient work for pupils					
6.	Reinforces attentive behaviour					
7.	Questions in all direction					
8.	Students interact appropriately					
9.	Chit-chat/noise controlled					
10.	Management of time					
	Total					
Total						

15. Skill Use of Black-board (BB)

Use of the black board seems to be an important part of teaching. This aid is present in almost all the schools in the country. It is a strong tool in the hands of the teacher. A teacher writes on the blackboard but she must remember that the matter written, gets embedded into the minds of the children. In general it is found, teachers under training are never told to organise the blackboard. They often scribble haphazardly for the sake of 'no-one' or nothing in particular.

A blackboard shows the title of the unit and focuses the students to the content. It also has important points of the content taught during the period, by the teacher. It also has an organized diagram with labeling if required, in the content taught. The teacher also arranges space for students to write or work on the board. In fact the blackboard has to be organized by the teacher just like a painter, who decides how the picture in his mind, is going to be transferred on the canvas.

(1) **Title of the unit written at correct place on Black-board:** After the student teacher gives a brief introduction, she comes to the topic of the unit. She says it aloud and simultaneously writes it on the board. Writing on the board focuses the student to the unit and he gets an idea of what is going to be taught in the class. It also stimulates his memory, incase he knows any thing on the subject.

(2) **Clear and organized Black-board:** The teacher organises the blackboard and its total space. A blackboard shows the title of the unit and focuses the students to the content. It also has important points of the content taught during the period, by the teacher. It also has an organized diagram with labeling (if required) on the content taught. The teacher also arranges space for students to write or work on the board.

(3) **Space organized on BB for student participation:** When teachers call students to

write on the board, there has to be space allotted for it. This type of student participation is used by teachers of mathematics, language, science ,geography etc.

(4) **Writing size visible to all;** Whenever any matter is written on the board by the teacher, it has to be legible and neat. This matter from the board, gets registered onto the minds of the student.

(5) **Relevant important points:** The teacher need not write definitions or answers on the board, but important points and spellings of difficult words, need to be written on the board. Many a times important points may be written by students as answers to the questions they had been asked.

(6) **Students answer-points on Black-board:** When students answer certain questions the important point is written by the teacher on the BB. This reinforces the content and makes the student feel 'great', that he has answered the question.

(7) **Creates interest/ helps understand unit:** Any important point taught by the teacher is written on the BB. Also answers to question, by the students are written on the BB. This creates interest in the unit taught and motivates the students to pay attention to the unit being taught. Many a times diagrams drawn on the BB, gives a better concept of the content Questions asked during the recapitulation are also answered easily with the support of the BB.

(8) **Forms concept, idea, relationship:** The blacboard work as a whole helps the student to understand, remember and clarify what he has learnt in the class. It also helps in determining the concept and the idea, from the matter taught. Simultaneously, the relationship in the contents or equations from the matter/statement of the content comes to the notice of the student

(9) **BB used for recapitulation:** Questions asked during the recapitulation are also answered easily with the support of the BB. Many a times diagrams drawn on the BB, gives a better concept of the content and the teacher asks questions based on it.

(10) **Assess students understanding:** As already said the questions on the blackboard work, helps the teacher teaching, assess the understanding of the unit by the students' answers and make him know the level of the students understanding of the topic he has taught.

(*Contd...*)

Skill Use of Black-board

S.No.	*Components of the skill*	*1*	*2*	*3*	*4*	*5*
1.	Title of the unit written at correct placę on BB					
2.	Clear and organized BB					
3.	Space organized on BB for student participation					
4.	Writing size visible to all					
5.	Relevant important points					
6.	Students answer points on BB					
7.	Creates interest/ helps understand unit					
8.	Forms concept, idea, relationship					
9.	BB used for recapitulation					
10.	Assess students understanding					
	Total					
Total						

Chapter 3

Review of Related Literature

If a teacher knows how to obtain more participation and involvement, he would probably be using it. If the teacher recognizes the teaching skill to be learned he begins to recognize the behaviours that make up the skill and the situational factors that dictate when it can be used.

Professional preparation of teachers, demand acquisition of specific skills of teaching, understanding of theories and principle of teaching, development of significant attitudes, towards teaching and profession by the teacher-trainees of all levels. Therefore teacher training programmes normally consists of mainly two aspects i.e. theory and practice teaching Becoming a teacher involves the complex act of teaching (by one person–the teacher) to a group of individually different set of students in a complex situation (the classroom). All efforts are in, to make teaching as easy as possible to achieve the expected change in behaviour from the students.

The microteaching modeling at CASE was tried out with written materials, lectures, demonstrations and discussions. The results were encouraging (Chaudasama-1971, Passi & Shah-1974).

The Department of Education in NCERT in 1975, studied the effectiveness of microteaching in collaboration with CASE (Centre of Advanced Study in Education), Baroda the Department of Education, University of Indore. The research has produced the need to modify the process of microteaching to suit Indian conditions. It is based on the presenting of skill, through the written materials, lectures, demonstration, discussions and not through films, video-tape recorders, cc television, as in the case of advanced technology model of microteaching used in UK, Australia etc.

Brown, et. al. (1975) have stressed that "microteaching will help you to sharpen and develop your teaching skills, it will help you to eliminate gross errors; and it will build up your confidence. It will not change your personality overnight; it will not solve all your teaching problems. It will not make you into a brilliant 'gifted teacher' – just a better one"

One of the intervention training-strategies is 'integration of teaching skills'. Das (1982) in India and Hargie (1978) in England successfully experimented the concept in their studies and the initial results have shown a trend towards improvement in teaching competence with the skill integration training following additive strategy.

Imparting training to in-service teachers, through the integration of teaching skills in microteaching, setting for improving their competency and enabling them to organize individually learnt skills into appropriate and if possible creative combinations, keeping in view the teaching task at hand is still an unexplored area and the effects of integration of skills through Summative and Additive strategies of microteaching is going to help a lot.

Ronald,T. Hymann (1965) and Sykes (1976) has said that teaching is a relationship which is established between three focus points in education: the teacher, the child and the subject. Teaching is the process by which the teacher brings the child and the subject together. The teacher and taught are active; the former is teaching and the latter is learning.

According to Thomas F. Green (1969) "teaching is an instant of human action, aimed at enhancing the human capacity for action". He says that the direct way to understand teaching is to grasp the difference between 'obedience to rule' and 'conformity to rule'. The most immediate way to understand this difference is to observe the ways in which learning a rule or learning to obey a rule of action differs from learning a habit.

According to Green every teaching involves learning while every-learning does not involve teaching. If learning is to be defined as a change in observable behaviour then it is not necessary that in the absence of observable change one should conclude that no learning has taken place. The learner may learn and yet decide not to manifest his new learning, through a change in his behaviour for the time being.

Mathur (1981) says that training is a process of modifying behaviours attitudes beliefs towards the desired direction and also a process of developing knowledge and skills through which organizational goals can be achieved successfully.

Pareek, U. (1970) talks about training, that it is aimed at learning a skill, a prescribed method of application of a technique. Education deals concerns basically with teaching to think in the presence of new situations

Das et al says that modeling which is an important component of microteaching helps in successful development of teaching skills, being practiced by the trainee. The major objective of modeling is to enable a teacher to exercise greater control over his own behaviour in classroom situation.

According to Stones and Morris (1972) training of teachers is a process of imitation in which the trainee, masters the teaching skills, performances, personality and attitudes through observation, imitation and practice.

Batley (1970) says that the trainee student should have a thorough understanding of theoretical basis of skills besides acquiring mastery over their use under microteaching.

According to Allen and Ryan (1969) microteaching is a real teaching, but in practice it is not so because of scaled down teaching situations in terms of time, number of students, content and skills to be learnt etc, It is far removed from the complexities of a classroom situation.

When we look at simulation technique, Unwin (1969), Bountree (1981) and Hills (1982) have observed that the student teachers play three different roles- as a teacher, as a student and as an observer. Each of them try to develop an identity with the actual classroom situation.

Copenland (1982) sees limitations to the benefits of simulation technique as he questions whether there is a change in the participant's behaviour due to simulated teaching activity.

When we talk about integration of skills in a regular classroom teaching practice Jangira and Singh (1982) says that it is the process through which a student teacher acquires the ability to perceive with precision the teaching situation, select and organize the component skills in a desired sequence to form meaningful pattern for realizing specific instructional objectives and use them with ease and fluency.

R.M.W. Travers (1973) says ultimately teaching is what the teacher does

Much work has to be yet done in improving the methods of teaching. Once the teacher understands what contributes to a good lesson she will clearly understand the use of skills as a useful teaching tool in the hands of the teacher.

Chapter 4

Planning Micro-lessons for Micro-teaching

Once the concept of microteaching is understood by the student teachers, they are asked to plan the micro-lesson. This part becomes very difficult or confusing for many students. They do not know how to plan the lesson. In this chapter we have given a general framework for a micro-lesson, followed by the lesson plan for a micro-lesson based on the *questioning skill.* This could be one way of planning the six minute lesson. However you could modify it according to your needs and achieve the insight in mastering the skills for being an expert teacher.

PLANNING A MICRO-LESSON

Whenever a unit/lesson is selected, one must take care to see that there is maximum scope to use the components of the skill (given in Ch. 2). The unit selected should be of about five minutes. You should keep in mind that, the unit is taught to the student-teachers (your colleagues) and you are not planning to teach the micro-lesson so that you can increase their general knowledge. This planning is for your ownself ie. You should be able, to understand your own teaching skills and reflect to understand where the skill achievement part is lagging. The ultimate goal is to master the skill. So you have to teach in such a way, that they rate your lesson, give you a feedback on it and with the help of this feedback you are able to re-plan your unit (the same unit) again. This re-planning should include a modification in the teaching i.e. it should be keeping the tips in mind given during the feedback. You must be in a position to score better when you re-teach. This will happen if your observers have given you the correct feedback verbally and through the rating scale. It is more important that you have taken it in the correct spirit and also understood where you could improve your unit for a re-teach session.

So, now we are in a position to plan the lesson as a regular lesson plan right from 'introduction to the 'achieving end of lesson' stage. Below is a general plan followed by a planned unit for the different skills.

Name of the Student teacher: ________

(Roll No): ________ Group No: ________

Skill: ________

Subject:________ Unit/Lesson:________ Class:

Date:________ Time: ________

OBJECTIVES

For the Student-Teacher (teaching):

1. To understand how to use only one skill in the total unit taught.

2. To plan the unit using the given skill.
3. To obtain feedback and understand where the use of the skill could be better.
4. To replan the same unit and modify the unit keeping in mind the feedback.
5. To re-teach the unit and understand the use of the skill.
6. To gain an insight of how best the skill is used with all its components.

For the Observers of the unit:

1. To understand the use of the rating scale after observing the taught micro-unit.
2. To understand the implications of the rating on the teacher, teaching the unit.
3. To understand how the skill-use can be enhanced.
4. To gain an insight of how best the skill is used with all its components.

Actual Steps in Microteaching Session

Step 1: Teaching Process Plan

Step 2: Marking and Feedback (Use of The Feedback Sheet Based on The Skill by Observers)

Step 3: Discussion and Implications of each marking/ step of the feedback

Step 4: Re-planning and Re-teaching(Modification of the Unit plan above in Step 1.Teaching Process Plan)

Step 5: Marking and Feedback (Use of The Re-

Feedback Sheet Based on The Same Skill)

Step 6: Discussion and Implications of each marking/ step of the Re-feedback

Step 7: Implication for

(1) teacher [student-teacher teaching]

(2) class of student teacher [observers]

Chapter 5

Questioning Skill

Planning Micro-lessons (Teaching Process Plan) for Microteaching

1. Name of the Student: **Anita Gomes**		Date: **10-11-2008**
Teacher	:	Class: **VII**
Roll No	: **43**	Group No: **III**
Subject	: **Geography**	Skill: **Questioning**
Unit/Lesson	: **Life in the Desert**	Time: **10.30 am**

2. Objectives:

For the Student-Teacher (teaching):

1. To understand how to use 'Questioning skill' in the total unit taught.
2. To plan the unit using the 'Questioning skill'.
3. To obtain feedback and understand where the use of the skill could be better.

For the Observers of the unit:

1. To understand the use of the rating scale for questioning (after observing the taught micro-unit).
2. To understand the implications of the rating by the observers on the teacher teaching the unit.
3. To understand how the skill-use, can be enhanced.
4. To gain an insight of how best the skill could have been used, with all its components.

3. (Step 1) Lesson Plan and Teaching:

Content	*Teacher Activities*	*Student Activities*	*Component of the Skill*
Title of the unit/Introduction:	Writes on the chalk board **"Life in the Desert"**		
Today we shall learn about "Life in the Desert"	What do you Know about a Desert?	Barren land Low rainfall Poor vegetation Hot temperature	Stimulating interest and thinking
	Very Good. Now all the answers you have given can be put under what we call "features of a desert"		
Features of the Desert:	What about the people?	The no. of people are less, no jobs, dressed from head to toe.	Seeking further information, providing lead/sequence of thought
	You know quite a few things about the desert.		
Land:	If we talk about the land it is full of sand, there is extensive gravel covering the plain. Sand dunes are also present in the desert.		Stimulating interest and thinking
	How are they formed?	By the wind	Seeking further information, providing lead/sequence of thought
Climate:	When we talk about the climate, we find it is hot, there is		

Content	*Teacher Activities*	*Student Activities*	*Component of the Skill*
	some rainfall and humidity is less.		Helps to under-stand
Vegetation and wild life:	The vegetation is less. Mostly it consists of scattered patches of grass and shrubs. Trees like palm, acacia, dates are found here. The leaves are modified to thorns and the stem is thick and fleshy to prevent loss of water. Do you know about the wild life here? Hyenas, desert foxes, snakes, lizards and insects are common.		Forms concept, relationship
	Do you know any other animal belonging to the desert?	Camel	Involves student participation
Recapitalation	Now lets see what you know about the desert. 1. Land? 2. Climate? 3. Vegetation? 4. Animals?	1. Dry, hot, sand and sand dunes. 2. Hot, dry, high temperature 3. Grass, palms, cactus 4. Camel, hyena, snakes	Involves student participation
	Good.		Assess students understanding

Step 2:

Marking and Feedback (Use of the Feedback Sheet Based on the Skill)

The observers after observing will rate the micro-lesson against the components in the feedback sheet. The rating is on the five point scale. The observers should be very objective while rating in order to rate correctly and have reasons for marking 1, 2, 3, 4 or 5. The correct feedback will help the teacher to understand where he/she needed to put in the questioning component into the unit. The feedback should be such that it should immediately make the teacher realize the shortcoming in the unit taught w.r.t. the components.

Below as a demonstration, we have given the rating scale **marked** by five student-teachers, observing the practice session of micro-teaching. We shall analyse the marking and give the feedback to the teacher teaching the micro-lesson and see how he utilizes these feedbacks in his re-planning of the same unit

(*Contd...*)

[First Rating Sheet Scored by Observer]

i. Name of the Student: **Anita Gomes** Date: **10-11-2008**
Teacher : **Teaching** Class: **VII**
Roll No : **43** Group No: **III**
Subject : **Geography** Skill : **Questioning**
Unit/Lesson : **Life in the Desert** Time: **10.30 am**

ii. Teach/Re-Teach

S. No.	*Components of the skill*	*1*	*2*	*3*	*4*	*5*
1.	Question are Clear, specific, relevant				√	
2.	Grammatically correct, accurate				√	
3.	Stimulating interest and thinking			√		
4.	Seeking further information, providing lead/sequence of thought		√			
5.	Helps to observe/understand		√			
6.	Forms concept, idea, relationship			√		
7.	Sufficient		√			
8.	Involves student participation			√		
9.	Have quality/assess students understanding.				√	
	Total		6	9	12	
	Total 27/45					

iii. Name of the Student : **Bela Singh** Roll N: **40**
Teacher : **Observing** Group No: **III**

[Second Rating Sheet Scored by Observer]

i. Name of the Student: **Anita Gomes** Date: **10-11-2008**
Teacher : **Teaching** Group No: **III**
Roll No : **43** Class: **VII**
Subject : **Geography** Skill: **Questioning**
Unit/Lesson : **Life in the Desert** Time: **10.30 am**

ii. Teach/Re-Teach

S. No.	*Components of the skill*	*1*	*2*	*3*	*4*	*5*
1.	Question are Clear, specific, relevant				√	
2.	Grammatically correct, accurate				√	
3.	Stimulating interest and thinking		√			
4.	Seeking further information, providing lead/sequence of thought		√			
5.	Helps to observe/understand		√			
6.	Forms concept, idea, relationship			√		
7.	Sufficient	√				
8.	Involves student participation		√			
9.	Have quality/assess students understanding.			√		
	Total	1	8	6	8	
	TOTAL 23/45					

iii. Name of the Student: **Chameli Das** Roll No: 20
Teacher **Observing** Group No: **III**

[Third Rating Sheet Scored by Observer]

i. Name of the Student: **Anita Gomes** Date: **10-11-2008**

Teacher : **Teaching** Group No: **III**

Roll No : **43** Skill: **Questioning**

Subject : **Geography** Class: **VII**

Unit/Lesson : **Life in the Desert** Time: **10.30 am**

ii. Teach/Re-Teach

S. No.	*Components of the skill*	*1*	*2*	*3*	*4*	*5*
1.	Question are Clear, specific, relevant			√		
2.	Grammatically correct, accurate				√	
3.	Stimulating interest and thinking		√			
4.	Seeking further information, providing lead/sequence of thought				√	
5.	Helps to observe/understand	√				
6.	Forms concept, idea, relationship		√			
7.	Sufficient	√				
8.	Involves student participation		√			
9.	Have quality/assess students understanding.			√		
	Total	2	6	6	8	
					TOTAL 22/45	

iii. Name of the Student: **Diana Williams** Roll No: **30**

Teacher: **Observing** Group No: **III**

[Fourth Rating Sheet Scored by Observer]

i. Name of the Student: **Anita Gomes** Date: **10-11-2008**

Teacher : **Teaching** Group No: **III**

Roll No : **43** Class: **VII**

Subject : **Geography** Skill: **Questioning**

Unit/Lesson : **Life in the Desert** Time: **10.30 am**

ii. Teach/Re-Teach

S. No.	*Components of the skill*	*1*	*2*	*3*	*4*	*5*
1.	Question are Clear, specific, relevant				√	
2.	Grammatically correct, accurate				√	
3.	Stimulating interest and thinking				√	
4.	Seeking further information, providing lead/sequence of thought			√		
5.	Helps to observe/understand		√			
6.	Forms concept, idea, relationship			√		
7.	Sufficient	√				
8.	Involves student participation		√			
9.	Have quality/assess students understanding.			√		
	Total	1	4	9	12	
						TOTAL 26/45

iii. Name of the Student: **Manoj Sharma** Roll No: **10**

Teacher: **Observing** Group No: **III**

[Fifth Rating Sheet Scored by Observer]

i. Name of the Student: **Anita Gomes** Date: **10-11-008**

Teacher : **Teaching** Group No: **III**

Roll No : **43** Class: **VII**

Subject : **Geography** Skill: **Questioning**

Unit/Lesson : **Life in the Desert** Time: **10.30 am**

ii. Teach/Re-Teach

S. No.	*Components of the skill*	*1*	*2*	*3*	*4*	*5*
1.	Question are Clear, specific, relevant				√	
2.	Grammatically correct, accurate				√	
3.	Stimulating interest and thinking		√			
4.	Seeking further information, providing lead/sequence of thought		√			
5.	Helps to observe/understand			√		
6.	Forms concept, idea, relationship			√		
7.	Sufficient	√				
8.	Involves student participation		√			
9.	Have quality/assess students understanding.				√	
	Total	1	6	6	12	
					TOTAL 25/45	

iii. Name of the Student: **Esha More** Roll No: **50**

Teacher: **Observing** Group No: **III**

Step 3 : Feedback and Implication's of each marked step

The analysis of the rating scale can be done in two ways.

(1) **Each individuals rating sheet analysis**

(2) **Each component and its rating by each individual** of the group of five. The highest marker can be asked why he has rated high on the component. Another student who has marked low can then be asked why he rated low and whoever has rated other than this can also give their reasons for rating whatever they have marked.

(The first part first i.e. ***individual rating sheet analysis***.)

In this method (**each individuals rating sheet analysis**), the feedback would be obtained by asking each individual about his rating scale and marks and the reasons for marking what he has rated-high, low or average. (for example analysing Bela's Rating Scale, the class teacher/supervisor sitting with the students may ask the questions regarding the rating or Bela herself can analyse her ratings before the class).

[First Rating Sheet Scored by Observer]

i. Name of the Student: **Anita Gomes** Date: **10-11-2008**

Teacher : **Teaching** Group No: **III**

Roll No : **43** Class: **VII**

Subject : **Geography** Skill: **Questioning**

Unit/Lesson : **Life in the Desert** Time: **10.30 am**

ii. Teach/Re-Teach

S. No.	*Components of the skill*	*1*	*2*	*3*	*4*	*5*
1.	Question are Clear, specific, relevant				√	
2.	Grammatically correct, accurate				√	
3.	Stimulating interest and thinking			√		
4.	Seeking further information, providing lead/sequence of thought		√			
5.	Helps to observe/understand		√			
6.	Forms concept, idea, relationship			√		
7.	Sufficient		√			
8.	Involves student participation			√		
9.	Have quality/assess students understanding.				√	
	Total		6	9	12	
	TOTAL 27/45					

iii. Name of the Student: **Bela Singh** Roll No : **40**

Teacher: **Observing** Group No: **III**

Bela: I have marked Anita 4 in S. No. 1 as I found her questions were clear, pinpointed and relevant to the topic. In S.No. 2 it is 4 again as they were grammatically correct and the student understands exactly what she wants to ask. Her questions were stimulating interest and thinking but I wanted her to ask more questions rather than tell us the details about the desert and so I rated her 3. The few questions she asked helped to provide information and lead but she did not use the answers to continue with the teaching of the unit. It was more explanation and so the students will naturally understand but it was important I thought to ask more questions and proceed so that you know how much your student knows, there will be more interaction and more enthusiasm and better learning . So I rated her 2. The teaching formed concepts so I gave a 3. There could have been more questions when she was telling about the land , vegetation, animals and other things. I did not rate her a 4 as the student participation would have been more if there were more questions. Whatever questions she asked were good questions explaining what she wanted to explain in the unit and so I have rated her a 4.

[Second Rating Sheet Scored by Observer]

i. Name of the Student: **Anita Gomes** Date: **10-11-2008**

Teacher : **Teaching** Group No: **III**

Roll No : **43** Skill: **Questioning**

Subject : **Geography** Class: **VII**

Unit/Lesson : **Life in the Desert** Time: **10.30 am**

ii. Teach/Re-Teach

S. No.	*Components of the skill*	*1*	*2*	*3*	*4*	*5*
1.	Question are Clear, specific, relevant				√	
2.	Grammatically correct, accurate				√	
3.	Stimulating interest and thinking		√			
4.	Seeking further information, providing lead/sequence of thought		√			
5.	Helps to observe/understand		√			
6.	Forms concept, idea, relationship			√		
7.	Sufficient	√				
8.	Involves student participation		√			
9.	Have quality/assess students understanding.			√		
	Total	1	8	6	8	
	TOTAL 23/45					

iii. Name of the Student: **Chameli Das** Roll No: **20**

Teacher: **Observing** Group No: **III**

Chameli: Marked 4 because the questions were clear specific and grammatically correct. The questions were less and could have stimulated more interest and thinking. They must be more, so I rated a 2. Similarly more questions would have created a lead to the unit and there could have been a flow of thoughts which did not happen as the teacher was lecturing more. So I rated her a 2. Her explanation helped to understand but the questions could have done this part so a 2. Whatever questions were asked it formed concepts and ideas but they should have been more questions. The questions were insufficient. She could have asked questions on climate, vegetation animals etc. but she did not do so I gave her a 1.Students were keen to participate but the teacher was keen to explain and finish the unit, so I rated her a 2. whatever questions were asked assessed students understanding but on account of a few questions I rated her a 3.

[Third Rating Sheet Scored by Observer]

i. Name of the Student: **Anita Gomes** Date: **10-11-2008**

Teacher : **Teaching** Group No: **III**

Roll No : **43** Class: **VII**

Subject : **Geography** Skill: **Questioning**

Unit/Lesson : **Life in the Desert** Time: **10.30 am**

ii. Teach/Re-Teach

S. No.	*Components of the skill*	*1*	*2*	*3*	*4*	*5*
1.	Question are Clear, specific, relevant			√		
2.	Grammatically correct, accurate				√	
3.	Stimulating interest and thinking		√			
4.	Seeking further information, providing lead/sequence of thought				√	
5.	Helps to observe/understand	√				
6.	Forms concept, idea, relationship		√			
7.	Sufficient	√				
8.	Involves student participation		√			
9.	Have quality/assess students understanding.			√		
	Total	2	6	6	8	
	TOTAL 22/45					

iii. Name of the Student: **Diana Williams** Roll No: **30**
Teacher: **Observing** Group No: **III**

Diana Williams: Questions were clear and specific but they probably could have been broken into shorter questions. They would be more clear. But I rated her 3. They were grammatically correct so a 4. Yes they were stimulating interest but the no. of questions were less so just 2. I found they were providing good lead to the unit and seeking information from the students so I rated a 4. The type of questions were same type and did not help to understand but they just came impulsively, so a 1. The no. of questions should have been more to form concepts and ideas through questions but more explanation was used so a 2. Insufficient questions so a 1. Students participation was less as the questions were broad and no. was less. So a 2. Quality of questions were good and they helped assess understanding so a 3.

[Fourth Rating Sheet Scored by Observer]

i. Name of the Student: **Anita Gomes** Date: **10-11-2008**

Teacher : **Teaching** Group No: **III**

Roll No : **43** Class: **VII**

Subject : **Geography** Skill**: Questioning**

Unit/Lesson: **Life in the Desert** Time: **10.30 am**

ii. Teach/Re-Teach

S. No.	*Components of the skill*	*1*	*2*	*3*	*4*	*5*
1.	Question are Clear, specific, relevant				√	
2.	Grammatically correct, accurate				√	
3.	Stimulating interest and thinking				√	
4.	Seeking further information, providing lead/sequence of thought			√		
5.	Helps to observe/understand		√			
6.	Forms concept, idea, relationship			√		
7.	Sufficient	√				
8.	Involves student participation		√			
9.	Have quality/assess students understanding.			√		
	Total	1	4	9	12	
	TOTAL 26/45					

iii. Name of the Student: **Manoj Sharma** Roll No: 10

Teacher: **Observing** Group No: **III**

Manoj Sharma: Questions were clear, relevant and grammatically correct so a 4 in each. It stimulated interest and so a 4 again. It was providing a lead and the students were understanding and answering so a 3 but more questions would have helped more. The teacher was too fast and did not wait to know whether the students were perceiving and understanding the question she was asking so a 2. It helped to form some concepts but questions should have been of the application type rather than direct. So a 3. Not sufficient no. of questions so a 1. More involvement could have been possible but the teacher preferred lecturing so a 2. More quality questions of the application type is needed to assess understanding so ok a 3

[Fifth Rating Sheet Scored by Observer]

i. Name of the Student: **Anita Gomes** Date: **10-11-2008**

Teacher : **Teaching** Group No: **III**

Roll No : **43** Class: **VII**

Subject : **Geography** Skill: **Questioning**

Unit/Lesson : **Life in the Desert** Time: **10.30 am**

ii. Teach/Re-Teach

S. No.	*Components of the skill*	*1*	*2*	*3*	*4*	*5*
1.	Question are Clear, specific, relevant				√	
2.	Grammatically correct, accurate				√	
3.	Stimulating interest and thinking		√			
4.	Seeking further information, providing lead/sequence of thought		√			
5.	Helps to observe/understand			√		
6.	Forms concept, idea, relationship			√		
7.	Sufficient	√				
8.	Involves student participation		√			
9.	Have quality/assess students understanding.				√	
	Total	1	6	6	12	
	TOTAL 25/45					

iii. Name of the Student: **Esha More** Roll No: -50

Teacher: **Observing** Group No: **III**

Esha More: The questions were very clear and grammatically correct, so a 4 is correct. It could have stimulated interested but the type of question and number of question was less, so a 2 and again a two for the same reason as more questions could have got more information from the students. It helped to observe and understand an ok-ok type so 3 and an ok-ok 3 for forming concepts idea and relationship. The number of questions had to be more, so a 1. It is all linked less questions less interactions, so a 2. Whatever questions were asked were very good and helped assess students understanding, so a 4.

We have seen the feedback above. This process of getting the feedback could be very long and time consuming. In a microteaching session the time allotted for this work expects the supervisor to complete the teach, re-teach sessions of all the student participant of the group. This includes the cycle of—plan, teach, feedback, replan, reteach and a refeedback. Another suitable method used and it works as good as individual feedback is to deal with the rating of each feedback component in totality. This means taking the feedback of every component from all the students one after another. This also helps the teacher waiting for the feedback, to note the shortcoming in each component of the skill or the good part of any component in her teaching. She can then plan her reteach session more easily and in a focused manner.

In this method of feedback, all the participants are alert and every individual is focused on the particular component under discussion (Please refer to the feedback sheet on pages 116–122. For understanding the analysis below.).

We shall now discuss and understand the second method **(Each component and its rating by each**

individual) of getting a feed back i.e. by taking a feedback of each component of the skill from all observers at a time one after another. Here one person from the group or supervisor could initiate the process of feedback. The process goes as follows.

Supervisor: (after Anita finished teaching her unit using the questioning skill) Anita please wait here, let us get a feedback from observers and see why they have rated you so. The first component: Were the questions **clear, specific and relevant?** Who has rated a 5? And Why? None of you? OK, so who has rated a 4?

Bela: I have marked Anita 4 in the first component as I found her questions were clear, pinpointed and relevant to the topic.

Chameli: I marked a 4 too, because the questions were clear specific.

Manoj: The Questions were clear and relevant, so a 4.

Esha: The questions were very clear, so a 4 is correct.

Supervisor: What have you marked Diana?

Diana*:* The Questions were clear and specific but they probably could have been broken into shorter questions. They could be more clear. So I rated her 3.

Supervisor: Okay, any other ratings? We shall proceed with the second component.

Grammatically correct, accurate: Who has rated a 5? Why? No one? Okay who has rated a 4? All of you ? why?

Chameli and Manoj: Because the questions were grammatically correct.

Supervisor: But why did you not rate her a 5?

Esha: The number of questions should have been more to know exactly if I should have given a 5 marks.

Supervisor: Okay, now the third component **'Stimulating interest and thinking'**: Who has rated a 5? Why? No one/ Who has rated a 4? Manoj? Ok, Why?

Manoj: I found it stimulated interest and so a 4 again.

Supervisor: OK, who has rated a 1? No one? A rating of 2? Why?

Chameli: The questions were less and could have stimulated more interest and thinking. They must be more, so I rated a 2.

Diana: Yes, they were stimulating interest but the number of questions were less, so just 2.

Esha: It could have stimulated interested but the type of question and number of question was less, so a 2.

Supervisor: Bela, what did you rate? A '3'? Why?

Bela: Her questions were stimulating interest and thinking but I wanted her to ask more questions rather than telling us the details about the desert and so I rated her 3.

Supervisor: Okay, now the fourth component ***'Seeking further information, providing lead/sequence of thought'***: Who has rated a 5?Why? No on ??? Who has rated a 4? Diana you did? Why?

Diana: The questions were seeking information and it was helping the lesson to progress one after another.

Supervisor: Who has rated a 3?

Manoj: The questions were seeking further information and leading the unit but there could be more questions.

Supervisor: Who has rated a two? All the others?

Bela, Chameli & Esha: Yes ma'am, questions should have been more and the lesson would have got a easier and faster lead.

Supervisor: Now let us go to the next component

'Helps to observe/ understand': Who has rated a 5; a 4? No one, again. OK, who has rated a 1? Diana?

Diana: The questions are too direct and do not make the listener use her mind to understand or visualize what she is saying.

Supervisor: A rating of 2? Three of you?

Bela: Same thing…, the question were too direct. There could have been questions at other places of the unit which would have helped to understand better.

Chameli: More questions would have made better understanding

Manoj: Same reason

Supervisor: Who has rated a 3? Esha you?

Esha: The questions she asked were okay, it helped to understand, but there could be more questions.

Supervisor: Okay, now we go to the the sixth component.***Forms concept, idea, relationship:*** Who has rated a 5? No? Who has rated a 4? OK, who has rated a 1? A rating of 2? Okay, Diana?

Diana: It could have formed a better concept, idea if there were questions of every thing explained in the unit.

Supervisor: Who has rated a 3?

Bela, Chameli, Manoj and Esha: All the questions asked formed ideas and concept, so we gave an average of 3, but there must be more questions.

Supervisor: Okay, now the seventh component is

Sufficient: Who has rated a 5?Why? Who has rated a 4? OK, who has rated a 1? All of you?

All: Yes because there were very few questions. This

unit could have been covered with a lot of different types of questions based on the unit.

Bela: I rated a 2 but she deserves only a 1.

Supervisor: Okay, Anita, you please note all the comments and try to improve your unit. Okay, now the eighth component **Involves student participation:** We will start with who has rated a 1? No one? Ok, who has rated a 2?All of you again?

All: There should have been more questions and then there would be more participation. Here only few students were motivated to answer.

Bela: I gave her a 3 because students were answering and they were eager to answer but the questions were few.

Supervisor: Okay, now the ninth component **Have quality/assess students understanding:** Who has rated a 5? Who has rated a 4?

Bela and Esha: Questions were there but at the recapitulation the questions were sufficient to assess students understanding.

Supervisor: OK, who has rated a 1? A rating of 2? Who has rated a 3?

We have seen the feedback in both the processes. Practically the second method was found more suitable. We shall now go to the next step where the teacher teaching replans the unit by including the expected corrections and modifying the unit taught at the first teach session and then teaches the <u>same unit</u> once again to the <u>same set</u> of students(colleagues).

Step 4:

Re-planning and Re-teaching (Modification of the Unit plan above in Step 1.Teaching Process Plan)

Planning (Re-Teach) micro-lessons for microteaching. (Questioning Skill):

Name of the Student: **Anita Gomes** — Date: **10-11-2008**
Teacher : — Group No: **III**
Roll No : **43** — Class: VII
Subject : **Geography** — Skill: **Questioning**
Unit/Lesson : **Life in the Desert** — Time: **10.30 am**

Content	*Teacher Activities*	*Student Activities*	*Component of the Skill*
Title of the unit/ Introduction:	Writes on the chalk board *"Life in the Desert"*		
Good morning chil-dren, today we shall learn about "Life in the Desert"	• What do you Know about a Desert? Very Good. Now all these answers you have given can be put under what we call "features of a desert"	Barren land Low rainfall Poor vegetation Hot temperature	Stimulating interest and thinking
Features of the Desert:	• What about the people? You know quite a few things about the desert.	The no. of people are less, no jobs, dressed from head to toe.	Seeking further information, providing lead/sequence of thought
Land:	If we talk about the land…. • What is it made of or what	It is full of sand, there is extensive gravel covering the	Helps to observe/understand

Content	Teacher Activities	Student Activities	Component of the Skill
	does it contain? • How are they formed?	plain. Sand dunes are also present in the desert.	Stimulating interest and thinking
Climate:	• What about the climate? Also the rainfall and humidity is less.	• By the wind we find it is hot,	Seeking further information, providing lead/sequence of thought
Vegetation and wild life:	• What about plants and vegetation? Yes you will see that the vegeta-tion is less. Mostly it consists of scattered patches of grass and shrubs. As you said trees like dates, palm, acacia are found here.	There are cactus and date trees	Seeking further information, providing lead/sequence of thought
	• You said cactus where are its leaves? The leaves are modified to thorns and the stem is thick and fleshy to prevent loss of water.	(No answer)	Helps to understand
	• Do you know about the wild life here? Yes besides there are Hyenas, desert foxes, snakes, lizards and insects which are common.	Camels are found in the desert.	Forms relationship Involves student participation
	• Do you know any other animal belonging to the desert? Ok people mostly keep them for their personal use.	Horses.	Involves student participation
Recapitulation	Now lets see what you know about the desert. • 1. Land? • 2. Climate? • 3. Vegetation? • 4. Animals? Good.	1. Dry, hot,sand and sand dunes. 2. Hot, dry, high temperature 3.Grass,palms, cactus 4.Camel, hyena, snakes	Assess students understanding

Step 5:

Marking and Re-feedback (Use Of The Re-Feedback Sheet Based on The Same Skill)

[First Rating Sheet Scored by Observer]

i. Name of the Student: **Anita Gomes** Date: **10-11-2008**

Teacher : **Teaching** Group No: **III**

Roll No : **43** Class: **VII**

Subject : **Geography** Skill: **Questioning**

Unit/Lesson : **Life in the Desert** Time: **10.30 am**

ii. Re-Teach

S. No.	*Components of the skill*	*1*	*2*	*3*	*4*	*5*
1.	Question are Clear, specific, relevant				√	
2.	Grammatically correct, accurate				√	
3.	Stimulating interest and thinking				√	
4.	Seeking further information, providing lead/sequence of thought				√	
5.	Helps to observe/understand			√		
6.	Forms concept, idea, relationship				√	
7.	Sufficient				√	
8.	Involves student participation					√
9.	Have quality/assess students understanding.					√
	Total			3	24	10
	TOTAL 37/45					

iii. Name of the Student: **Bela Singh** Roll No: **40**

Teacher: **Observing** Group No: **III**

[Second Rating Sheet Scored by Observer]

1. Name of the Student: **Anita Gomes** Date: **10-11-2008**
Teacher : **Teaching** Group No: **III**
Roll No : **43** Class: **VII**
Subject : **Geography** Skill: **Questioning**
Unit/Lesson: **Life in the Desert** Time: **10.30 am**

2. Re-Teach

S. No.	*Components of the skill*	*1*	*2*	*3*	*4*	*5*
1.	Question are Clear, specific, relevant					√
2.	Grammatically correct, accurate				√	
3.	Stimulating interest and thinking				√	
4.	Seeking further information, providing lead/sequence of thought				√	
5.	Helps to observe/understand				√	
6.	Forms concept, idea, relationship					
7.	Sufficient				√	
8.	Involves student participation				√	
9.	Have quality/assess students understanding.				√	
	Total			3	28	5
	TOTAL 36/45					

3. Name of the Student: **Chameli Das** Roll No: **20**
Teacher: **Observing** Group No: **III**

[Third Rating Sheet Scored by Observer]

1. Name of the Student: **Anita Gomes** Date: **10-11-2008**

Teacher : **Teaching** Group No: **III**

Roll No : **43** Class: **VII**

Subject : **Geography** Skill: **Questioning**

Unit/Lesson : **Life in the Desert** Time: **10.30 am**

2. Re-Teach

S. No.	*Components of the skill*	*1*	*2*	*3*	*4*	*5*
1.	Question are Clear, specific, relevant				√	
2.	Grammatically correct, accurate				√	
3.	Stimulating interest and thinking				√	
4.	Seeking further information, providing lead/sequence of thought				√	
5.	Helps to observe/understand				√	
6.	Forms concept, idea, relationship			√		
7.	Sufficient					√
8.	Involves student participation					√
9.	Have quality/assess students understanding.					√
	Total			3	20	15
	TOTAL 38/45					

3. Name of the Student: **Diana Williams** Roll No: **30**

Teacher: **Observing** Group No: **III**

[Fourth Rating Sheet Scored by Observer]

1. Name of the Student: **Anita Gomes** Date: **10-11-2008**

Teacher : **Teaching** Group No: **III**

Roll No : **43** Class: **VII**

Subject : **Geography** Skill: **Questioning**

Unit/Lesson : **Life in the Desert** Time: **10.30 am**

2. Re-Teach

S. No.	*Components of the skill*	*1*	*2*	*3*	*4*	*5*
1.	Question are Clear, specific, relevant				√	
2.	Grammatically correct, accurate				√	
3.	Stimulating interest and thinking				√	
4.	Seeking further information, providing lead/sequence of thought				√	
5.	Helps to observe/understand			√		
6.	Forms concept, idea, relationship			√		
7.	Sufficient				√	
8.	Involves student participation				√	
9.	Have quality/assess students understanding.				√	
	Total			6	28	
	TOTAL 34/45					

3. Name of the Student: **Manoj Sharma** Roll No: **10**

Teacher: **Observing** Group No: **III**

[Fifth Rating Sheet Scored by Observer]

1. Name of the Student: **Anita Gomes** Date: **10-11-2008**

Teacher : **Teaching** Group No: **III**

Roll No : **43** Class: **VII**

Subject : **Geography** Skill: **Questioning**

Unit/Lesson : **Life in the Desert** Time: **10.30 am**

2. Re-Teach

S. No.	*Components of the skill*	*1*	*2*	*3*	*4*	*5*
1.	Question are Clear, specific, relevant				√	
2.	Grammatically correct, accurate				√	
2.	Grammatically correct, accurate				√	
3.	Stimulating interest and thinking				√	
4.	Seeking further information, providing lead/sequence of thought				√	
5.	Helps to observe/understand				√	
6.	Forms concept, idea, relationship				√	
7.	Sufficient				√	
8.	Involves student participation				√	
9.	Have quality/assess students understanding.				√	
	Total	1	6	6	12	
	TOTAL 36/45					

3. Name of the Student: **Esha Moore** Roll No: **50**

Teacher: **Observing** Group No: **III**

Step 6:

Discussion and Implications of each marking and re-feedback

We shall analyse the re-feedback sheet using the second method **(Each component and its rating by each**

individual) Every individuals feedback will rate each feedback component and we shall see a totality. This means taking the feedback of every component from all the students one after another. This also helps the teacher waiting for the feedback, to note how well she has improved from the previous feedback. It forms a part of helping the teacher understand how to use the particular skill and the role of the components. Also a type of an insight dawns on the student teacher when this step of feedback at the re-teach session occurs. If any component needs to be treated in a better way that too is obtained in the feedback. Every teacher who is able to correct herself from the feedback and take the feedback in a positive manner, however negative the rating may be, learns from the shortcoming in each component of the skill. The skill she uses is going tø help her be 'a good technically qualified teacher'.

At this point in feedback, all the participants are alert and every individual is focused on the particular component of the skill rather than the unit taught, under discussion. (Please refer to the feedback sheet on pages 124-128 above for understanding the analysis below.)

Once again one person from the group or supervisor could initiate the process of re-feedback. The process goes on as follows.

> **Supervisor:** (after Anita has finished teaching her unit using the questioning skill) Anita please wait here, let us get a feedback again from your observers and see why they have rated you so. The first component: Were the questions ***clear, specific and relevant***? Who has rated a 5? And Why? Chameli you did rate a five?
>
> **Chameli:** I marked a 5, because the questions were clear specific and they were an improvement on the first time.

Supervisor: OK so who has rated a 4? All the remaining students? Well, well now let us see the reason.

All Bela, Manoj, Esha & Diana: The unit was much better and very clear and there was a lot of improvement. She asked a lot of short clear questions.

Supervisor: Okay we shall proceed with the second component.

Grammatically correct, accurate: Who has rated a 5? Why? No one? Okay who has rated a 4? All of you? why?

Chameli and Manoj: Because the questions were grammatically correct.

Supervisor: But why did you not rate her a five?

Esha: We wanted to leave some scope if they could be any better.

Supervisor: Okay now the third component ***'Stimulating interest and thinking'*** :Who has rated a 5?Why? No one/ Who has rated a 4? All of you again?

Manoj, Chameli,Diana: The large no on questions stimulated interested

Esha & Bela: Her questions were stimulating interest as she got most of the details of the unit from the students by her questions.

Supervisor: Okay now the fourth component **'Seeking further information, providing lead/ sequence of thought':** Who has rated a 5? No one ??? Who has rated a 4? All of you again?

Diana: The questions were seeking information and it was helping the lesson to progress one after another very easily.

Manoj: The questions were seeking further information and leading the unit and there were more questions.

Bela, Chameli & Esha: Yes ma'am, questions were more and the lesson became easier and it got a quick and faster lead.

Supervisor: Now let us go to the next component **'Helps to observe/understand':** Who has rated a 5? A 4? Ok Chameli, Diana and Esha

Diana, Chameli & Esha: The questions were stimulating and thought provoking. The listener uses his mind to understand or visualize what she is saying.

Bela & Manoj: The increase in the number of questions have helped to understand better.

Supervisor: Okay now we go to the the sixth component. **Forms concept, idea, relationship:** Who has rated a 5? No? Who has rated a 4? Bela and Esha?

Bela, Esha: There were more questions. All the questions asked formed ideas and concepts better than when the unit was taught before

Chameli, Manoj, Diana: It could have formed a better concept, idea if there were questions pertaining to the students idea of a desert and asking them questions with the thought of forming a concept. So we rated a 3.

Supervisor: Okay now the seventh component is **Sufficient:** Who has rated a 5?Why? **Bela:** A lot of questions were asked and it was better than previous lesson

All the others: We gave a 4 as there could be questions on concept forming, observation and better understanding

Supervisor: Okay Anita you please note all the comments again and try to improve your unit further. Okay now the eighth component **Involves student participation:** We will start with who has rated a 1?

No one? Ok who has rated a 2? No one? 3? 4? Chameli, Manoj and Esha?

Chameli, Manoj and Esha: There were a lot of questions and so naturally participation will be more.

Bela & Diana: Also the type of participation involved students and they were eager to answer.

Supervisor: Okay now the ninth component **Have quality/assess students understanding:** Who has rated a 5?

Bela & Diana: Questions were plenty and the recapitulation had sufficient questions to assess students understanding

Chameli, Manoj and Esha: We have rated a 4 as there could be more questions in the recap section.

We have seen the planning and the re-planning as well as feedback and re-feedback. Again the replanning continues till the teacher teaching attains perfection of the skill.

Step 7:

Implication for 1) teacher [student-teacher teaching]

The teacher teaching in the beginning does not realize how to use the components of the skill while teaching. She plans her lesson as best as she can, like a good teacher does for her daily classwork. Initially she is also confused as to how any lesson/unit can be taught in five to six minutes.

Once she teaches the unit, it is the feedback and the correct rating by her colleagues that make her realize where she could have been better at using the component. The first feedback gives her an understanding of the rating and how it could be enhanced. She mentally makes a note of all the comments and shortcomings in her lesson and when she replans the unit her focus shifts to getting a high rating from her colleagues rather than thinking that she is trying to teach them and increase their information and general knowledge of the unit. So, now she plans the unit, taking care of the components of the skill thereby unconsciously stretching towards mastering the skill. She delivers her replanned unit and waits patiently for the feedback. This feedback is bound to score high, if the student-teacher has taken care to understand the first feedback and replan her unit. The high score also boosts the student to further understand the re-feedback and the use of the components of the skill. (In the case of Anita above, she has scored a 3 in two components at the refeedback session in component 5 and 6 i.e. 'Helps to observe/understand' and 'Forms concept, idea, relationship'. She is bound to think about it and how she can score high. (Also she is going to observe other student-teachers lesson and understand from her feedback rating scale and others too, how the skill can be used towards perfection.) Slowly... by such practice the student gets an insight, how best the particular skill can be used and then it comes naturally when she is teaching (in a proper regular class) a proper lesson from the syllabus.

Implication for 2) the class of student teacher who are observers.

The observers have the rating scale sheet and observe the unit. They then rate the teacher against each component. They relate the unit to the component as well as each action reaction that took place during the teaching session. Accordingly they rate on the five point scale and are also conscious and knowing why they have rated a 5 or a 3 or a 1 etc. She/he is able to justify the rating and is very objective and judicious in her markings. The observer simultaneously realizes where the unit could have been explored or taught in a different manner so that the component is used accurately. They are able to understand each of the components well and also what type of question needed to be used, for a particular step in the unit. What is important is that rating her colleague, also influences, her own planning of her unit which she is going to teach to her class of colleagues during the microteaching sessions.

Hence it will be seen that not only the teaching session helps to master the skills but the observing session too is a contributor to understanding how well can the skill be mastered.

Chapter 6

Activity Planning

A Micro-lesson for skills based on

1. **Explanation**
2. **Audio-visual aids**
3. **Stimulus Variation**
4. **Reinforcement**

Activity: Planning A Micro-lesson for the skill based on: *Explanation Skill*

Actual Steps in Microteaching Session

Make one person the Supervisor from the group who will manage the feedback of the marking and discussion following it.

The Supervisor then picks up the order of teaching and gives each person their turn-number to teach. When one person teaches the others become the Observers.

The Supervisor then distributes the rating sheets to be scored by the Observers

In the meantime the person who is going to teach the micro lesson gets ready to teach the group.

Step 1:

Teaching Process Plan for 'Explanation' skill

Step 1:

Teaching Process Plan for 'Explanation' skill

Lesson Plan and teaching:

Name of the Student teacher (Roll No): ______________

Group No: ______________

Skill: ______________

Subject: ______________ Unit/Lesson: __________ Class:

Date: ______________ Time: ______________

Objectives:

For the Student-Teacher (teaching):

1. To understand how to use only the *'Explanation'* skill in the total unit taught.
2. To plan the unit using the *'Explanation'* skill.
3. To obtain feedback and understand where the use of *'Explanation'* could be better.
4. To replan the same unit and modify the unit keeping in mind the feedback.
5. To re-teach the unit and understand the use of the *'Explanation'* skill.
6. To gain an insight of how best the *'Explanation'* skill is used with all its components.

For the Observers of the unit:

1. To understand the use of the rating scale after observing the taught micro-unit.
2. To understand the implications of the rating on the teacher teaching the unit.
3. To understand how the skill use can be enhanced.

   To gain an insight of how best the skill is used with all its components.

Title of the unit:

Content	*Teacher Activities*	*Student Activities*	*Component of the Skill*

Step 2:

Marking and Feedback (Use of the Feedback Sheet Based on the Skill of 'Explanation' by Observers)

Step 3:

Discussion and Implications of each marking/step of the feedback

After the teaching of the micro-lesson is over, the Supervisor asks the observers to score on the rating scale.

Every Student-observer will score/mark the above rating scale, understanding and ready to explain the score.

The Supervisor will then discuss the scoring on each component of the skill. The Teacher will note the comments and proceed to replan the unit.

Step 4:

Re-planning and Re-teaching(Modification of the Unit plan above in Step 1.Teaching Process Plan)

The same teacher replans the unit keeping in mind the feedback. (In the meantime another student prepared with her micro lesson can be called on to teach and a feedback obtained in a similar manner. This will save time of the group.)

Once the teacher with the above plan is ready with the reteach session she will teach the unit to the group

Step 5:

Marking and Feedback (Use of the Re-Feedback Sheet Based on the Same Skill Explanation)

The Supervisor distributes the rating scale of the Re-Teach session and asks the same observers to rate the Teacher on the same lesson (replanned) unit.

Skill : Explanation Re-Teach session

Name of Teacher (Teaching Class)						
S.No.	*Components*	*1*	*2*	*3*	*4*	*5*
1.	Introductory statement					
2.	Clear voice, change in tone and pitch					
3.	Continuous and fluent					
4.	Relevant to context					
5.	Covering essential points					
6.	Using explaining links					
7.	Simple relevant examples					
8.	Body movement and gestures					
9.	Made clear,using AV aids					
10.	Used concluding statement					
	Total					
Name of Teacher (Observing Class)						

Step 6

Discussion and Implications of each marking/step of the Re-feedback

Once again the Supervisor after the re-teaching of the micro-lesson is over, asks the observers to score on the rating scale.

Every Student-observer will score/mark the above (re-teach) rating scale, understanding and ready to explain the score.

The Supervisor will then discuss the scoring on each component of the skill of explanation. The Teacher will note the comments and understand where the unit has improved or still needs improving and proceed to replan the unit

Step 7:

Implication for 1) teacher [student-teacher teaching]

Any teacher in the beginning of teaching does not realize how to use the components of the Explanation skill.. She plans her lesson as best as she can, like a good teacher does for her daily classwork. Initially she is also confused as to how any lesson/unit can be taught in five to six minutes.

Once she teaches the unit, it is the feedback and the correct rating by her colleagues that make her realize where she could have been better at using the component. The first feedback gives her an understanding of the rating and how it could be enhanced. She mentally makes a note of all the comments and shortcomings in her lesson and when she replans the unit her focus shifts to getting a higher rating from her colleagues rather than thinking that she is trying to teach them and increase their information and general knowledge of the unit. So, now she plans the unit, taking care of the components of the skill of Explanation, thereby unconsciously building towards mastering the skill. She delivers her replanned unit and waits patiently for the feedback. This feedback is bound to score high, if the student-teacher has taken care to understand the first feedback and replan her unit. The high score also boosts the student to further understand the re-feedback and the use of the components of the skill.

Slowly... by such practice the student gets an insight, how best the particular skill can be used and then it comes naturally when she is teaching (in a proper regular class) a proper lesson from the syllabus.

Implication for 2) the class of student teacher who are observers.

The observers use the rating scale sheet, after observing the unit. They then rate the teacher against each component of the Explanation skill. They relate the unit to the component as well as each action reaction that took place during the teaching session. Accordingly they rate on the five point scale and are also conscious and knowing why they have rated a 5 or a 3 or a 1 etc. She/he is able to justify the rating and is very objective and judicious in her markings. The observer simultaneously realizes where the unit could have explored or taught in a different manner so that the component is used accurately. She is able to understand each of the components well and also how to modify the explanation in the unit. What is important is that rating her colleague, also influences, her own planning of the personal unit which she is going to teach her class of colleagues during the microteaching sessions.

Hence it will be seen that not only the teaching session helps to master the skills but the observing session too is a contributor to understanding how well can the skill be mastered.

Activity: Planning A Micro-lesson for the skill based on: *Audio-visual aids Skill*

Actual Steps in Microteaching Session

Make one person the Supervisor from the group who will manage the feedback of the marking and discussion following it.

The Supervisor then picks up the order of teaching and gives each person their turn-number to teach. When one person teaches the others become the Observers.

The Supervisor then distributes the rating sheets to be scored by the Observers

In the meantime the person who is going to teach the micro lesson gets ready to teach the group.

Step 1:

Teaching Process Plan for 'Audio-visual aids' skill

Lesson Plan and teaching:

Name of the Student teacher (Roll No): ______________

Group No: ______________

Skill: ______________

Subject: ______________ Unit/Lesson:______ ______ Class:

Date: ______________ Time: ______________

Objectives:

For the Student-Teacher (teaching):

1. To understand how to use only the *'Audio-visual aids'* skill in the total unit taught.
2. To plan the unit using the *'Audio-visual aids* skill.
3. To obtain feedback and understand where the use of *'Audio-visual aids'* could be better.
4. To replan the same unit and modify the unit keeping in mind the feedback.
5. To re-teach the unit and understand the use of the *'Audio-visual aids'* skill.
6. To gain an insight of how best the *'Audio-visual aids'* skill is used with all its components.

For the Observers of the unit:

1. To understand the use of the rating scale after observing the taught micro-unit.
2. To understand the implications of the rating on the teacher teaching the unit.

3. To understand how the skill use can be enhanced.
4. To gain an insight of how best the skill is used with all its components.

Title of the unit:

Content	*Teacher Activities*	*Student Activities*	*Component of the Skill*

Step 2:

Marking and Feedback (Use of the Feedback Sheet Based on the Skill of 'Audio visual aids' by Observers)

Step 3:

Discussion and Implications of each marking/step of the feedback

After the teaching of the micro-lesson using the 'Audio-visual aid skill' is over, the Supervisor asks the observers to score on the rating scale.

Every Student-observer will score/mark the above rating scale, understanding and ready to explain the score.

The Supervisor will then discuss the scoring on each component of the skill. The Teacher will note the comments and proceed to replan the unit.

Step 4:

Re-planning and Re-teaching(Modification of the Unit plan above in Step 1. Teaching Process Plan)

The same teacher replans the unit keeping in mind the feedback. (In the meantime another student prepared with her micro lesson can be called on to teach and a feedback obtained in a similar manner. This will save time of the group.)

Once the teacher with the above replan is ready with the reteach session she will teach the unit to the group

Step 5:

Marking and Feedback (Use of The Re-Feedback Sheet Based on The Same Skill Explanation)

The Supervisor distributes the rating scale of the Re-Teach session and asks the same observers to rate the Teacher on the same lesson (replanned) unit

Skill: Audio Visual Aid Re-Teach session

Name of Teacher (Teaching Class)						
S.No.	*Components*	*6*	*7*	*8*	*9*	*10*
11.	Clear, specific picture					
12.	Size					
13.	Relevant to topic					
14.	Stimulating					
15.	Creates interest and thinking					
16.	Helps understand unit					
17.	Seeking further information					
18.	Forms concept, idea, relationship					
19.	Students participation					
20.	Assess students understanding					
	Total					
Name of Teacher (Observing Class)						

Step 6:

Discussion and Implications of each marking/step of the Re-feedback

Once again the Supervisor after the re-teaching of the micro-lesson is over, asks the observers to score on the rating scale.

Every Student-observer will score/mark the above (re-teach) rating scale, understanding and ready to explain the score.

The Supervisor will then discuss the scoring on each component of the skill of Audio visual aid. The Teacher will note the comments and understand where the unit has improved or still needs improving and proceed to replan the unit

Step 7:

Implication for 1) teacher [student-teacher teaching]

Any teacher in the beginning of teaching does not realize how to use the components of the Audio Visual Aid skill. She plans her lesson as best as she can, like a good teacher does for her daily classwork. Initially she is also confused as to how any lesson/unit can be taught in five to six minutes.

Once she teaches the unit, it is the feedback and the correct rating by her colleagues that make her realize where she could have been better at using the component. The first feedback gives her an understanding of the rating and how it could be enhanced. She mentally makes a note of all the comments and shortcomings in her lesson and when she replans the unit her focus shifts to getting a higher rating from her colleagues rather than thinking that she is trying to teach them and increase their information and general knowledge of the unit. So, now she plans the unit, taking care of the components of the skill of Audio Visual Aid, thereby unconsciously building towards mastering the skill. She delivers her replanned unit and waits patiently for the feedback. This feedback is bound to score high, if the student-teacher has taken care to understand the first feedback and replan her unit. The high score also boosts the student to further understand the re-feedback and the use of the components of the skill.

Slowly .... by such practice the student gets an insight, how best the particular skill can be used and then it comes naturally when she is teaching (in a proper regular class) a proper lesson from the syllabus.

Implication for 2) the class of student teacher who are observers.

The observers use the rating scale sheet, after observing the unit. They then rate the teacher against each component of the Audio Visual Aid skill. They relate the unit to the component as well as each action reaction that took place during the teaching session. Accordingly they rate on the five point scale and are also conscious and knowing why they have rated a 5 or a 3 or a 1 etc. She/he is able to justify the rating and is very objective and judicious in her markings. The observer simultaneously realizes where the unit could have explored or taught in a different manner so that the component is used accurately. She is able to understand each of the components well and also how to modify the explanation used, using the Audio Visual Aid in the unit. What is important is that rating her colleague, also influences, her own planning of the personal unit which she is going to teach her class of colleagues during the microteaching sessions.

Hence it will be seen that not only the teaching session helps to master the skills but the observing session too is a contributor to understanding how well can the skill be mastered.

Activity: Planning A Micro-lesson for the skill based on: *Stimulus Variation Skill*

Actual Steps in Microteaching Session

Make one person the Supervisor from the group who will manage the feedback of the marking and discussion following it.

The Supervisor then picks up the order of teaching and gives each person their turn-number to teach. When one person teaches the others become the Observers.

The Supervisor then distributes the rating sheets to be scored by the Observers

In the meantime the person who is going to teach the micro lesson gets ready to teach the group.

Step 1:

Teaching Process Plan for 'Stimulus Variation' skill

Lesson Plan and teaching:

Name of the Student teacher (Roll No): ____________

Group No: __________

Skill: __________

Subject: ____________ Unit/Lesson:__________ Class:

Date: ____________ Time: ____________

Objectives:

For the Student-Teacher (teaching):

1. To understand how to use only the *'Stimulus Variation'* skill in the total unit taught.
2. To plan the unit using the *'Stimulus Variation'* skill.
3. To obtain feedback and understand where the use of *'Stimulus Variation'* could be better.

4. To replan the same unit and modify the unit keeping in mind the feedback.
5. To re-teach the unit and understand the use of the *'Stimulus Variation'* skill.
6. To gain an insight of how best the *'Stimulus Variation'* skill is used with all its components.

For the Observers of the unit:

1. To understand the use of the rating scale after observing the taught micro-unit.
2. To understand the implications of the rating on the teacher teaching the unit.
3. To understand how the skill use can be enhanced.
4. To gain an insight of how best the skill is used with all its components.

Title of the unit:

Content	*Teacher Activities*	*Student Activities*	*Component of the Skill*

Step 2:

Marking and Feedback (Use of the Feedback Sheet Based on the Skill of 'Stimulus Variation' by Observers)

Step 3:

Discussion and Implications of each marking/step of the feedback

After the teaching of the micro-lesson using the 'Stimulus Variation skill' is over, the Supervisor asks the observers to score on the rating scale.

Every Student-observer will score/mark the above rating scale, understanding and ready to explain the score.

The Supervisor will then discuss the scoring on each component of the skill. The Teacher will note the comments and proceed to replan the unit.

Step 4:

Re-planning and Re-teaching (Modification of the Unit plan above in Step 1.Teaching Process Plan)

The same teacher replans the unit keeping in mind the feedback. (In the meantime another student prepared with her micro lesson can be called on to teach and a feedback obtained in a similar manner. This will save time of the group.)

Once the teacher with the above replan is ready with the reteach session she will teach the unit to the group.

Step 5:

Marking and Feedback (Use of the Re-Feedback Sheet Based on The Same Skill Stimulus Variation)

The Supervisor distributes the rating scale of the Re-Teach session and asks the same observers to rate the Teacher on the same lesson (replanned) unit.

Skill: Stimulus Variation Re-Teach session

Name of Teacher (Teaching Class)						
S.No.	*Components*	*6*	*7*	*8*	*9*	*10*
11.	Body movements					
12.	Gestures					
13.	Change in tone					
14.	Pause					
15.	Audio-visual aids					
16.	Teacher-class interaction					
17.	Teacher-pupil interaction					
18.	Focusing pupil's attention (verbal/gesture)					
19.	Pupil movement-physical participation.					
	Total					
Name of Teacher (Observing Class)						

Step 6:

Discussion and Implications of each marking/step of the Re-feedback

Once again the Supervisor after the re-teaching of the micro-lesson using 'Stimulus Variation Skill' is over, asks the observers to score on the rating scale.

Every Student-observer will score/mark the above (re-teach) rating scale, understanding and ready to explain the score.

The Supervisor will then discuss the scoring on each component of the skill of stimulus variation. The Teacher will note the comments and understand where the unit has improved or still needs improving and proceed to replan the unit.

Step 7:

Implication for 1) teacher [student-teacher teaching]

Any teacher in the beginning of teaching does not realize how to use the components of the Stimulus Variation Skill skill.. She plans her lesson as best as she can, like a good teacher does for her daily classwork. Initially she is also confused as to how any lesson/unit can be taught in five to six minutes.

Once she teaches the unit, it is the feedback and the correct rating by her colleagues that make her realize where she could have been better at using the component. The first feedback gives her an understanding of the rating and how it could be enhanced. She mentally makes a note of all the comments and shortcomings in her lesson and when she replans the unit her focus shifts to getting a higher rating from her colleagues rather than thinking that she is trying to teach them and increase their information and general knowledge of the unit. So, now she plans the unit, taking care of the components of the skill of Stimulus Variation Skill, thereby unconsciously building towards mastering the skill. She delivers her replanned unit and waits patiently for the feedback. This feedback is bound to score high, if the student-teacher has taken care to understand the first feedback and replan her unit. The high score also boosts the student to further understand the re-feedback and the use of the components of the skill.

Slowly ... by such practice the student gets an insight, how best the particular skill can be used and then it comes naturally when she is teaching (in a proper regular class) a proper lesson from the syllabus.

Implication for 2) the class of student teacher who are observers.

The observers use the rating scale sheet, after observing the unit. They then rate the teacher against each component of the Stimulus Variation Skill skill. They relate the unit to the component as well as each action reaction that took place during the teaching session. Accordingly they rate on the five point scale and are also conscious and knowing why they have rated a 5 or a 3 or a 1 etc. She/he is able to justify the rating and is very objective and judicious in her markings. The observer simultaneously realizes where the unit could have explored or taught in a different manner so that the component is used accurately. She is able to understand each of the components well and also how to modify the explanation used, using the Stimulus Variation Skill in the unit. What is important is that rating her colleague, also influences, her own planning of the personal unit which she is going to teach her class of colleagues during the microteaching sessions.

Hence it will be seen that not only the teaching session helps to master the skills but the observing session too is a contributor to understanding how well can the skill be mastered.

Activity: Planning A Micro-lesson for the skill based on: *Reinforcement Skill*

Actual Steps in Microteaching Session

Make one person the Supervisor from the group who will manage the feedback of the marking and discussion following it.

The Supervisor then picks up the order of teaching and gives each person their turn-number to teach. When one person teaches the others become the Observers.

The Supervisor then distributes the rating sheets to be scored by the Observers.

In the meantime the person who is going to teach the micro lesson gets ready to teach the group.

Step 1:

Teaching Process Plan for 'Reinforcement' skill

Lesson Plan and teaching:

Name of the Student teacher (Roll No): ______________

Group No: ______________

Skill: ______________

Subject: ______________ Unit/Lesson:______________ Class:

Date:______________ Time: ______________

Objectives:

For the Student-Teacher (teaching):

1. To understand how to use only the *'Reinforcement'* skill in the total unit taught.
2. To plan the unit using the *'Reinforcement'* skill.
3. To obtain feedback and understand where the use of *'Reinforcement'* could be better.
4. To replan the same unit and modify the unit keeping in mind the feedback.
5. To re-teach the unit and understand the use of the *'Reinforcement'* skill.
6. To gain an insight of how best the *'Reinforcement'* skill is used with all its components.

For the Observers of the unit:

1. To understand the use of the rating scale after observing the taught micro-unit.
2. To understand the implications of the rating on the teacher teaching the unit.
3. To understand how the skill use can be enhanced.
4. To gain an insight of how best the skill is used with all its components.

Title of the unit:

Content	*Teacher Activities*	*Student Activities*	*Component of the Skill*

Step 2:

Marking and Feedback (Use of the Feedback Sheet Based on the Skill of 'Reinforcement' by Observers)

Step 3:

Discussion and Implications of each marking/step of the feedback

After the teaching of the micro-lesson using the 'Reinforcement skill' is over, the Supervisor asks the observers to score on the rating scale.

Every Student-observer will score/mark the above rating scale, understanding and ready to explain the score.

The Supervisor will then discuss the scoring on each component of the skill. The Teacher will note the comments and proceed to replan the unit.

Step 4:

Re-planning and Re-teaching (Modification of the Unit plan above in Step 1. Teaching Process Plan)

The same teacher replans the unit keeping in mind the feedback. (In the meantime another student prepared with her micro lesson can be called on to teach and a feedback obtained in a similar manner. This will save time of the group.)

Once the teacher with the above replan is ready with the reteach session she will teach the unit to the group.

Step 5:

Marking and Feedback (Use of the Re-Feedback Sheet Based on The Same Skill Reinforcement)

The Supervisor distributes the rating scale of the Re-Teach session and asks the same observers to rate the Teacher on the same lesson (replanned) unit.

Skill : Reinforcement Re-Teach session

Name of Teacher (Teaching Class)						
S.No.	*Components*	*6*	*7*	*8*	*9*	*10*
11.	Positive reinforcement(Good, Correct, Yes, Fine, Well done, Go on, Carry on, Go Ahead)					
12.	Student deserved					
13.	Stimulating					
14.	Providing lead/seeking further information					
15.	Positive non-verbal reinforcement (Nods, smiles, friendly look)					
16.	Writing pupils response on board					
17.	Students participation					
18.	Repetition of correct response was suitable					
19.	Wrong response weakened or broken					
20.	Teacher-pupil interaction					
	Total					
Name of Teacher (Observing Class)						

Step 6:

Discussion and Implications of each marking/step of the Re-feedback

Once again the Supervisor after the re-teaching of the micro-lesson using 'Reinforcement Skill' is over, asks the observers to score on the rating scale.

Every Student-observer will score/mark the above (re-teach) rating scale, understanding and ready to explain the score.

The Supervisor will then discuss the scoring on each component of the skill of Reinforcement. The Teacher will note the comments and understand where the unit has improved or still needs improving and proceed to replan the unit.

Step 7:

Implication for 1) teacher [student-teacher teaching]

Any teacher in the beginning of teaching does not realize how to use the components of the Reinforcement Skill.. She plans her lesson as best as she can, like a good teacher does for her daily classwork. Initially she is also confused as to how any lesson/unit can be taught in five to six minutes.

Once she teaches the unit, it is the feedback and the correct rating by her colleagues that make her realize where she could have been better at using the component. The first feedback gives her an understanding of the rating and how it could be enhanced. She mentally makes a note of all the comments and shortcomings in her lesson and when she replans the unit her focus shifts to getting a higher rating from her colleagues rather than thinking that she is trying to teach them and increase their information and general knowledge of the unit. So, now she plans the unit, taking care of the components of the skill of Reinforcement Skill, thereby unconsciously building towards mastering the skill. She delivers her replanned unit and waits patiently for the feedback. This feedback is bound to score high, if the student-teacher has taken care to understand the first feedback and replan her unit. The high score also boosts the student to further understand the re-feedback and the use of the components of the skill.

Slowly ... by such practice the student gets an insight, how best the particular skill can be used and then it comes naturally when she is teaching (in a proper regular class) a proper lesson from the syllabus.

Implication for 2) the class of student teacher who are observers.

The observers use the rating scale sheet, after observing the unit. They then rate the teacher against each component of the Reinforcement Skill. They relate the unit to the component as well as each action reaction that took place during the teaching session. Accordingly they rate on the five point scale and are also conscious and knowing why they have rated a 5 or a 3 or a 1 etc. She/he is able to justify the rating and is very objective and judicious in her markings. The observer simultaneously realizes where the unit could have explored or taught in a different manner so that the component is used accurately. She is able to understand each of the components well and also how to modify the explanation used, using the Reinforcement Skill in the unit. What is important is that rating her colleague, also influences, her own planning of the personal unit which she is going to teach her class of colleagues during the microteaching sessions.

Hence it will be seen that not only the teaching session helps to master the skills but the observing session too is a contributor to understanding how well can the skill be mastered.

References

Agrawal, Rashmi, (2009), *Educational Technology, Management and Evaluation*, Shipra Publications, Delhi.

Aubertine, Horace E., (1967), *'The use of microteaching in training supervising teachers'.*

Brown, G.A., (1975), *'Microteaching: A Programme of Teaching Skills'*, Methen and Co. Ltd. London.

Chauhan, S.S,. (2002) (p. 131), *Innovations in Teaching-Learning Process.*

Cooper, James M., (1967-Paper), 'Microteaching as a pre internship training technique for the development of specific teaching skills.'

Cooper, James M., (1967), 'Developing Teaching Skills through Microteaching'.

Dahiya, Surinder S., (2004), *Educational Technology: Towards Better Teacher Performance,* Shipra Publications, Delhi.

Das, R.C., Passi B.K. and Singh, L.C., (1976), *'A Study of The Effectiveness of Microteaching in training of Teachers'*, Deptt. of Edu. NIE, NCERT, Delhi.

Dosajh, N.L., (1975), *'Modification of Teacher Behaviour Through Micro Teaching'*, Sterling Publishing House, New Delhi.

Hargie, O.D.W., Dickson, D.A. and Tittmar H.D., (1978), 'Mini Teaching-An Extension of the Microteaching Format', *British Journal of Teacher Education*, (pp. 113-118).

Hargie, O.D.W. & Maidment, P.A., *'Microteaching in Perspective'*, Blackstaff Press Ltd, Dundonald.

Jangira, N.K. and Singh, Ajit, (1982), *'Core Teaching Skills: Microteaching Approach'*, Publication Division, NCERT, New Delhi.

Kalyanpurkar, Shushila, (1986), 'The Effect of microteaching on the teaching competence of inservice teachers and its impact on pupils attainment and pupils liking'.

Kallenbach Warren, (1986-paper), "The effectiveness of microteaching in the preparation of elementary Intern teachers".

Mukhopadhyaya, Marmar, (2004), *Educational Technology: Knowledge Assessment,* Shipra Publications, Delhi.

Naik, Dolaganjan, (1989), 'A Study of the different Models of integration exercise of teaching skills learned high through microteaching upon teaching effectiveness & teacher attitude.'(5) pp. 17-20.

Passi, B.K. and Singh, Ajit, (1980), 'Micro analysis of Teaching Skills, An illustration of Prompting', *Journal of Indian Education.*

Ruhela, S.P. (2002), '*Educational Technology*'.

Sabarwal, V.K., 'Effectiveness of microteaching with planned integration, training following summative model and microteaching without planned integration training on the general teaching competencies of teacher trainees.'

Sampath, K., Paneerselvam, A., Santhanam S., (1998), '*Introduction to Educational Technology*'.

Saxena, Swarup, N.R.,Oberoi, S.C., (2002), pp. 318-341. '*Technology of Teaching*'.

Sedgewick, L.K. and Misfield, (1967), '*Microteaching–New Tool for a New Program-Industrial Arts and vocational Education*'.

Singh, L.C., Sharma, R.D., (2002) '*Micro Teaching: Theory & Practice*'.

Srivastava, H.S., (2010), *Curriculum and Methods of Teaching,* 2nd Rev. Edition, Shipra Publications, Delhi.

Stones, E. & Morris, S., (1972), '*Teaching practice-Problems and Perspectives,* Methen and Co. London.

Tara Chand, (1999), (p. 105), '*Educational Technology*'.

Thakker, R.C., (1985), 'Study of the effect of different microteaching skills upon general teaching competency of primary teacher trainees'.

Travers, R.N.W., (1973), '*Second Handbook of Research on Teaching*', Rand McNally, Chicago.